FASHION PROMOTION

BUILDING A BRAND THROUGH MARKETING
AND COMMUNICATION

BLOOMSBURY VISUAL ARTS

LONDON · NEW YORK · OXFORD · NEW DELHI · SYDNEY

BLOOMSBURY VISUAL ARTS
Bloomsbury Publishing Plc
50 Bedford Square, London, WC1B 3DP, UK
1385 Broadway, New York, NY 10018, USA

BLOOMSBURY, BLOOMSBURY VISUAL ARTS and the Diana logo are
trademarks of Bloomsbury Publishing Plc

First published in Great Britain 2012 by AVA Publishing SA
Reprinted by Bloomsbury Visual Arts 2017, 2019

Cover design: Pony Ltd.
Cover image © Poppy Roberts

A catalogue record for this book is available from the British Library.

Library of Congress Cataloging-in-Publication Data
Moore, Gwyneth.
Basics Fashion Management 02: Fashion Promotion: Building a brand
through marketing and communication / Gwyneth Moore p. cm.
Includes bibliographical references and index.
ISBN: 9782940411870 (pbk. :alk. paper)
eISBN: 9782940447473
1. Internet marketing. 2. Public relations. 3. Fashion merchandising.
HF5415.1265 .M557 2012
10 9 8 7 6 5 4 3 2 1

ISBN: PB: 978-2-9404-1187-0
    ePDF: 978-2-9404-4747-3

Series: Basics Fashion Management

Printed and bound in Great Britain

To find out more about our authors and books visit www.bloomsbury.com
and sign up for our newsletters.

1

1 JAYNE HICKS

This striking image was styled
and photographed by fashion
promotion student Jayne Hicks.

TABLE OF CONTENTS

1

INTRODUCTION

Fashion promotion is a fast-growth industry that has had to adapt to a massive shift in the way in which we all communicate. In recent times this has primarily been driven by the explosion of social and digital media platforms and channels. As print advertising revenues decline, magazines and newspapers go out of print, and citizen journalism takes over, the promotion of a fashion brand has become a far more multi-faceted and varied exercise than it once was.

Consumer knowledge of fashion and manufacturing has increased and small designers, manufacturers and retailers can now compete with larger, more established organizations. The playing field has become more level, but this has made it necessary for brands to be able to develop and execute a unique offering or experience for their customers.

This book looks at the ways in which fashion brands are reaching out to consumers and making their designs, products and services available to as many relevant and interested customers as possible. The opportunities afforded by online platforms are discussed, along with how the visual representation of a brand can heavily influence how customers feel and respond to it.

We also look at fashion illustration, photography and video, and how to work with professionals in these industries as well as the very focused and targeted work of fashion PR and media relations.

Collaboration is a 'buzzword' of the twenty-first century, and we explore some of the various ways in which people are collaborating and partnering for the greater good of brands, both large and small.

Fashion promotion and communication is continually evolving and being driven towards a more customer-centric, personalized way of providing information and opportunities to buy fashion. Some of the predictions for future promotion and purchasing opportunities are also explored throughout the book.

1 'THE TEDS'

The promotion of fashion is still about image, but street style and styling have become increasingly relevant and powerful when selling brands.

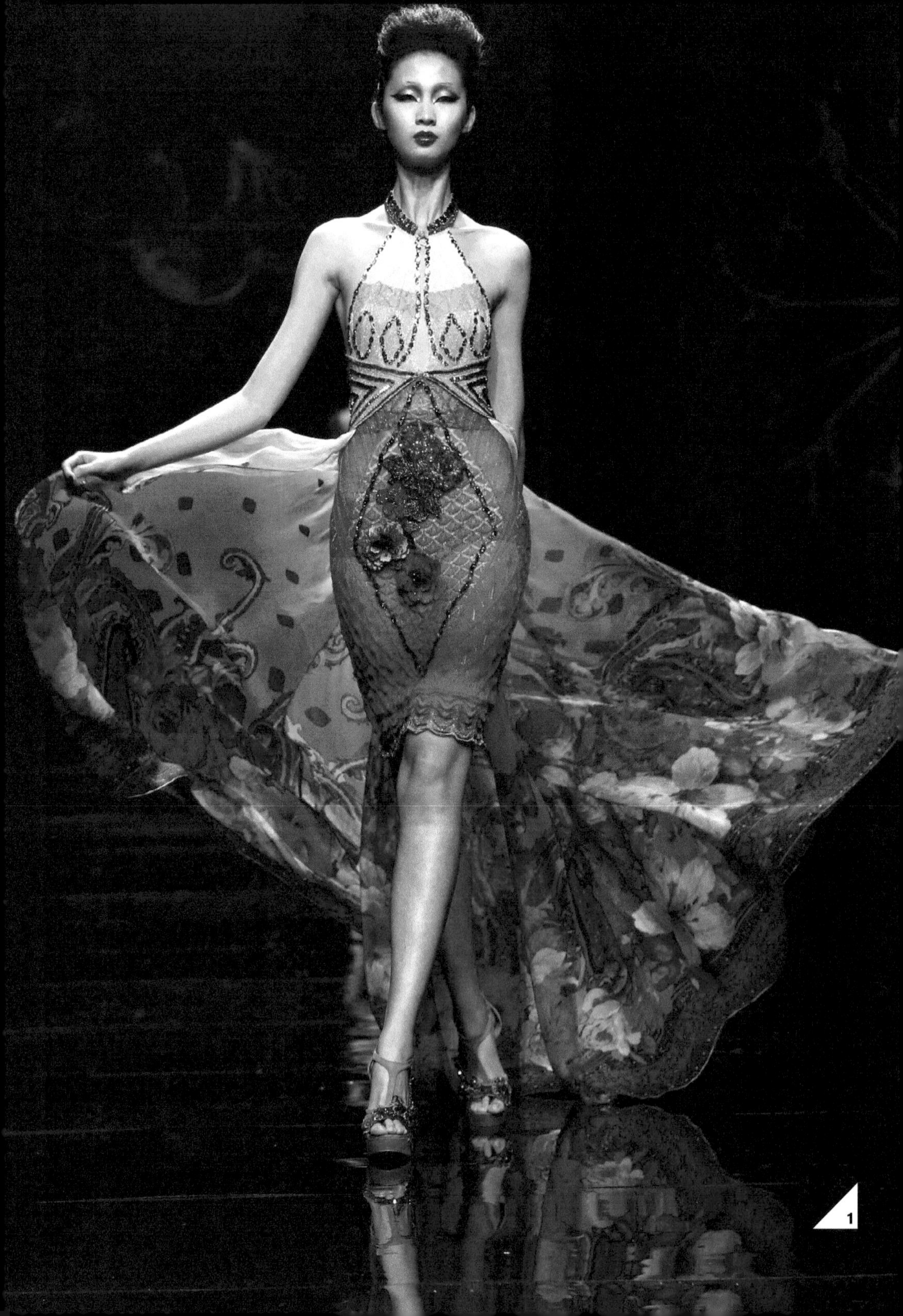

1

INDUSTRY AND CONTEXT

1

The fashion industry is tremendously fast-paced, consuming new ideas and trends at an astonishing rate. What is considered fashionable one day can be seen as *passé* the very next. It is vital for any brand to keep ahead of these changes and successfully communicate their ideas and designs to build a loyal following of customers.

Global and economic factors influence what the world consumes and wears, and fashion brands must consider the global audience more than ever before. With new online sales channels, the marketplace has become broader and more diverse, but also increasingly competitive.

In this chapter we will take a look at how fashion brands can face the challenge of communicating with this wide, international audience, and how they can stand out to an increasingly savvy and demanding consumer.

1 DENG HAO

Fashion weeks are no longer the preserve of New York, Milan, Paris and London – this colourful creation by Deng Hao was showcased during Beijing Fashion Week in 2011.

Brand building

Building a strong identity is key for any fashion brand. It allows you to present a clear idea of what you are selling, the concept and ethos behind it, the underlying principles of the brand and the way in which it is sold. These elements create a background for the brand and a picture of what it is about – what it stands for, its attributes and values, and ultimately why the customer will want to buy into it. A brand is a company's personality and what it hopes to represent to the customer.

There is, of course, a need for strong design and quality construction. However, without a brand name, identity, value and equity, it is challenging for a customer to firstly locate the brand, and then to understand and identify with what is being sold to them. Many believe that a brand is about a logo and the visual identity only, but it is about much more than this and can include references to heritage and history, luxury, lifestyle and celebrity endorsement.

Brand identity should be built around a number of elements, including the reasons the brand was developed and what the target audience is looking for; this is determined by conducting market research. It is also about how the products or services are devised, produced and made available and, ultimately, what the brand wants to be known or 'famous' for.

It is crucial to understand that there can be little promotion or communication of a brand if there is no story to tell or background regarding why it exists in the first place.

'What I did as a fashion designer for both Gucci and Yves Saint Laurent was to create a character and then costume that character throughout her life.'
Tom Ford

1　MVM

Designer Michelle McGrath chose a simple, text-based logo, and used muted tones with an elegant pose to represent her brand MVM.

M

MICHELLE VICTORIA
McGRATH

Brand building

The brand still matters

While routes to market have developed considerably and communications channels are now many and varied, there remains a need to offer a strong 'story' or background to a brand that compels the customer to find out more. It is therefore crucial to have a clear vision of what the brand should mean to the customer.

Consumers gather information about brands from a number of different sources. These will include looking at the visual identity or logo, the stores and clothes themselves, as well as all of the other elements of the brand and its background that the company presents to the audience. We learn about Topshop, for example, from the stores, the website, the products, adverts, blogs, fashion weeks, online campaigns, Twitter and collaborations. All of these elements combine to build a clear picture of what the brand stands for, believes, and strives to create.

It is not enough just to create great fashion; a brand has to create a complete story behind its ideas so that the consumer can both differentiate it from the competition and feel an affinity with it.

1 TOPSHOP BRANDING

High-street giant Topshop presents each element of the brand consistently across all customer contact points, from shop window, to store interior and web presence.

1

HIGH-STREET BRANDS

By looking at high-street retailers such as Topshop and H&M, you can surmise that part of each brand's focus is to have an overall mass-market appeal to a mainly young audience. But there is also evidence of a strong aspirational design focus for both retailers, seen through collaborations with reputable designers such as Versace (H&M) and Celia Birtwell (Topshop). They have also each established endorsements with celebrity style icons Madonna (H&M) and Kate Moss (Topshop). Both brands understand the need to appeal to consumers on a number of levels, but also that all elements of the brand must complement each other.

'When you think of the blur of all the brands that are out there, the ones you believe in and the ones you remember, like Chanel and Armani, are the ones that stand for something. Fashion is about establishing an image that consumers can adapt to their own individuality.'
Ralph Lauren

Brand building

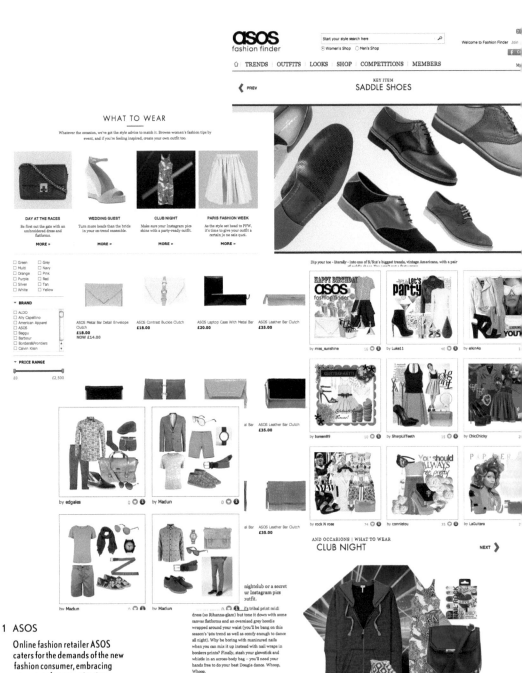

1 ASOS

Online fashion retailer ASOS
caters for the demands of the new
fashion consumer, embracing
new ways of communicating
brands and products.

Adapting for the new consumer

With global influences, market conditions, the explosion of digital communication, a more demanding consumer and greater levels of competition, it is becoming increasingly difficult for fashion brands, large and small, to compete. Differentiators that enable brands to have a unique selling point (USP) are becoming harder to define, as local markets develop to include global audiences, and luxury brands continue to expand their offering to mass markets.

However, the growth in communication channels and access to two-way conversations with the customer means it is still possible to create a strong, focused brand that appeals to the modern consumer. More than ever before, brands are required to listen to the customer and respond accordingly, but this also means that product development can be efficiently targeted, and marketing and promotional campaigns can be bespoke and responsive.

Fashion collections and the people and creativity behind them are gaining more attention from the consumer, and the industry is still attracting enthusiastic apprentices and interns across most disciplines. The fashion and creative industries are receiving more business kudos from governments and in some areas, increased levels of recognition and funding from official bodies. This can be seen with the publication of the **UK fashion industry report**. The challenge is to ensure the market remains customer-focused as well as creative and cutting edge, embracing varied audiences while still remaining commercially viable.

Market research, creativity, strong brand stories, well-developed products, and responsiveness to customer feedback are all key to the creation of a brand that is appealing to the new consumer.

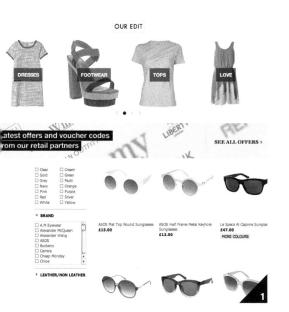

UK FASHION INDUSTRY REPORT

In 2010 the British Fashion Council commissioned a report into the value of the UK fashion industry. The report analysed the industry's profit, as well as fashion education, fashion marketing and fashion media.

The study concluded that the fashion industry at that time was worth £21 billion/$32 billion a year to the UK economy, and as much as £37 billion/$57 billion when related businesses were taken into account.

Part of the focus of this report was to give the government the impetus to invest more readily in the fashion industry. The report also made recommendations for the future – including the provision of better business training for fledgling designers and providing support once businesses are up-and-running.

The shifting communications landscape

At a time when information bombards the consumer at every turn, it has become increasingly challenging for any brand to be heard above the noise.

A hundred years ago the majority of consumers would have bought goods from local suppliers and would have perhaps been aware of a handful of international brands. As communication became easier with the development of television and radio, alternatives to local brands were offered and consumers were targeted by the new forms of advertising that came with these developments in communication.

The development of the Internet has brought about the most significant shift in the way in which we consume information about brands and also how we are influenced by them. The availability of information through digital channels, and the ease with which we can share it with each other through social media, means that we no longer necessarily believe everything a brand tells us. We now demand more information about brands, we expect them to engage with us – almost on a one-to-one basis – and we look to online word-of-mouth feedback, above traditional sales patter.

The speed at which information travels has increased dramatically and we no longer need to rely only on 'official' sources such as newspapers and magazines. We have often already heard the news through our own personal channels of communication, before it is officially released.

The fast-moving fashion industry, with its need to share ideas and imagery, engage with the customer on an emotional level, and to keep ahead of new trends, has embraced this new age of communication with enthusiasm.

SOCIAL NETWORKING

According to a recent paper produced by global digital market intelligence organization comScore, 64.2 million US smartphone users accessed social networking sites or blogs on their mobile devices at least once in Dec 2011, with more than half of these accessing social media almost every day.

While mobile social networking users showed the highest propensity to read posts from people they knew personally, more than half of those in the US also reported reading posts from brands, organizations and events.

1   BURBERRY SS12

Burberry is considered a digital trailblazer for translating and communicating what appears on the catwalk into easily consumable information, and spreading brand awareness.

The shifting communications landscape

Before the digital revolution

To fully understand the impact that recent advances in digital communication have had on fashion, it is necessary to know how things were done before the sharing of information became so widespread, instant and accessible.

There were a number of traditional routes for a new fashion brand, large or small, to be seen by the customer. A label and brand would be devised based on the vision of the fashion designer. These would be interpreted to create visuals or **marketing materials** for the brand. If these proved successful, the brand might exhibit at fashion weeks around the world, hire a PR agency, meet with the press and buyers, and their profile would start to build.

With a large enough budget, a designer could advertise in fashion and lifestyle magazines and newspapers, and work with the media on interviews and features. The audience connected with at this first tier – editors, PR, buyers and fashion week teams – would be relatively small and once their support was gained, progress would be fairly smooth.

MARKETING MATERIALS

A brand's basic marketing materials often include the following:
× A lookbook, which is a collection of individual photographs of each item in a collection, clearly showing the garments.
× A brochure, which may include more conceptual and styled images of a collection, along with detailed brand and designer information and branding.
× A media or press pack, which can include all of the above along with a press release, press-specific images and contact details for media and buyers.

1 BRITISH VOGUE APP

Fashion brands use many tools to communicate with the consumer. British *Vogue* created an iPad app to offer its readers an alternative way to access the publication.

1

New approaches

Now, although a label and brand is still devised by the designer in much the same way, it is likely that the lookbook, brochure, press information and imagery will all be accessible in one location – the website.

If a designer exhibits at fashion week, anyone, anywhere in the world can view it, online via live streaming. A PR agency may still be engaged to make use of their experience and media contacts, but a designer can equally engage with influential bloggers and websites. An e-commerce website can be set up to enable the sale of the designs directly to the public, or collaboration with an existing online retailer could also be established to introduce the label to a larger market.

The availability of digital channels, allowing real-time communication, enables instant customer contact and feedback. It allows a brand to quickly let people know what they are doing and when. This is powerful and enables the smallest brand to compete, to some extent, with much larger ones. If a designer is good at creating a brand and communicating what it stands for and offers, then the impact has the potential to reach far and wide.

The shifting communications landscape

The new era of sharing

If a consumer wanted to gain an insight into New York style in the past, they would have to visit the city themselves or wait for the latest magazine to cover the trends there. In-house researchers at fashion brands would have been conducting their own research, often travelling the globe and taking their own photographs, or employing people at different locations to carry out the research for them.

Since fashion blogs and street style websites, such as Facehunter and The Locals, have become more mainstream, consumers across the globe are able to see what others are wearing and share their experience of style in their own locality. The insight that bloggers and street-style commentators give the consumer into what others are wearing has a strong influence on what consumers want to wear. This sharing of fashion and style trends online has also made it considerably easier for brands to continually research street style and ensure that they stay in touch with what their customers want.

Bloggers, by their nature, are all about sharing information, thoughts and opinions with others. They also share information with each other, so while there may be some competition between them, as information spreads throughout the network so too does their reach and profile, as well as that of their followers.

WARDROBE INSPIRATION

A more level playing field

The result of this new era of sharing is that the playing field for fashion communication and promotion has become more level. If a designer has Internet access, good content, something to say and, of course, a good idea or product, then they have the potential to compete with bigger brands that have significantly bigger budgets.

They still have to consider what they want their brand to be famous for – high quality, bespoke, cutting-edge designs, or mass-market appeal clothes for everyday wear? They also need to consider how they want their brand to stand out, and even if they gather a loyal following, customers will only return if they have a good experience and like the products. If a designer invests the time needed to create a good product, a well-developed brand story and a strong understanding of what the customer is looking for, there are now greater opportunities to reach consumers than ever before.

1   MY-WARDROBE.COM

My-wardrobe.com was set up by Jane Curran in 2006 and is one online fashion retailer providing a range of services to its customers. It is an online luxury fashion boutique, which also offers style advice, editorial features, interviews and industry updates.

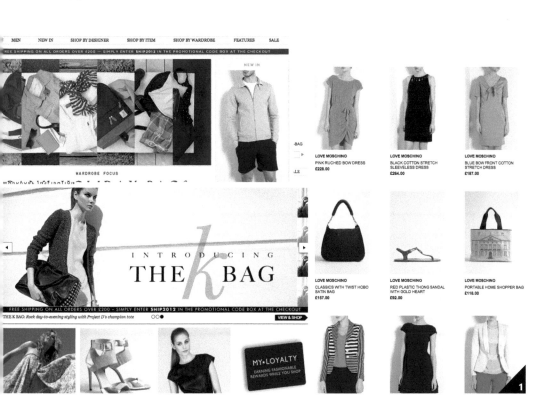

1

Global market changes

1

Luxury labels were once the preserve of the rich and famous, but brands such as Dior and Burberry have begun to capitalize on a wider market share, and are reaching a much broader audience. Previously struggling to compete with high-street brands both on turnover and market visibility, luxury brands have recently launched accessory ranges, cosmetics, perfumes and more affordable diffusion labels. These retain the essence of the brand, but cater for a wider audience.

These more accessible but aspirational luxury products have attracted a following of fans, and while some may argue they have compromised the exclusivity of the brands, they have undoubtedly impacted turnover positively. LVMH Group, currently the world's largest owner of luxury brands, has seen significant growth in recent times, as have rivals such as Burberry.

Emerging markets in Asia, particularly China, have also helped luxury brands to increase their market share as the desire to own a piece of fashion from the likes of Chanel, Hermès or Lanvin is still strong across the world. As emerging markets continue to flourish economically, owning luxury goods has become more realistic for hordes of new fashion consumers.

Changing attitudes

Coverage of poor working conditions in third world 'sweatshops' has impacted the way in which consumers perceive fashion brands. Increased awareness of the way in which people in other countries live and work has forced some brands to clean up their act when it comes to commissioning cheap labour to manufacture their goods.

Soaring cotton prices have also affected the cost of producing clothing and many retailers have predicted price rises in fashion goods. This can be seen as a positive, as it could potentially lead to an overall improvement in the quality of garment production.

The age of throw-away, cheap fashion may never completely leave us, but perhaps through a combination of increased social conscience, greater environmental awareness, and closer connections between consumers and brands, we will see a more evolved industry that places a higher value on quality over quantity.

1 PLAZA 66, SHANGHAI

This luxury shopping centre in Shanghai, China, demonstrates the increased presence of luxury brands in emerging markets. Brands such as Christian Dior, Fendi, Hermès, Louis Vuitton, and Prada can all be found here.

The new fashion consumer

As we've seen, the twenty-first century fashion consumer has more information at their fingertips than previous generations. Today, if the consumer wants to buy fashion, they can source exactly what they're looking for instantly, online, at any time of the day or night. They can see the latest trends and global influences, and share what they find with friends and contacts.

Many online fashion retailers provide delivery within 24-hours, but more recently same-day delivery services have become available in some cities, allowing consumers to have the items they have purchased in a matter of hours.

Global brands have been providing their own online stores for some time, but new e-commerce sites, such as farfetch.com, provide access to stock from small boutiques around the world, allowing customers to buy from one central location. Sites such as this can also offer price benefits, allowing consumers to take advantage of differing exchange rates. Some online stores also provide details of where celebrities and fashion icons have sourced their wardrobe items, and where less costly equivalents can be found.

1

New demands – choosing their own channels

As fashion consumers are increasingly bombarded with information by brands and labels all vying for their attention, they are becoming more adept at filtering through the information and researching what they are looking for. For a fashion brand, there is pressure to provide the right information in the right format at the right time, for the right audience.

Brands are therefore now creating their own content, so that many brand websites have become editorially focused, or have become portals for developing communities to engage with customers on multiple levels. This can include creating trend and style advice editorial sections, competitions, online communities that encourage shopper input and feedback, blogger collaborations and much more.

Style Insider for River Island is one high-street brand creating magazine-style fashion and news content to help sell the brand in a new format.

The consumer's decision to buy is influenced by many things, not least because there are now so many competing sources of information. The consumer however also now expects, perhaps even demands, to be communicated with on a number of levels.

Despite online developments, many retailers agree that fashion will continue to be supplied through multiple channels – department stores, high-street outlets, boutiques, discount outlets, dedicated online sites, collaborative online offerings and supermarkets. The physical experience of shopping for fashion will remain an important and irreplaceable activity for many consumers.

Traditional 'bricks and mortar' retail outlets will need to develop if they are to compete with online channels by providing higher levels of customer service along with increased product and purchasing information in-store.

1 THE PHYSICAL
EXPERIENCE

For many consumers, the physical experience of shopping in-store cannot be replaced by online retailers.

The new fashion consumer

The rise of citizen journalism

The accessibility of the web and of blog platforms such as Wordpress, Blogger and Typepad, has opened up the floodgates for individual content creation. More of us see the potential of sharing our thoughts and opinions with others. For some, this has become a lucrative and successful venture, offering opportunities to not only share on their own blogs, but to collaborate with fashion brands, writers, and designers.

Blogging has taken on a significant role in the fashion industry on many levels, creating citizen commentators, opinion formers, influencers and trendsetters. It also has a number of guises, from bloggers that offer a personal insight into what they are wearing, such as What Katie Wore, to commentary on celebrity outfits, on Couture Candy, and street style sites, such as The Sartorialist.

Some fashion bloggers, such as Bryan Boy and Tavi Gevinson, have become celebrities in their own right, and are invited to catwalk shows, influencing collections and being asked for their feedback. Through blogging, individuals are given a voice, sometimes on a global scale. Ultimately, if they are successful, this allows them to create a position of respect and influence within the fashion industry.

1

It is, however, worth noting that those that are successful in making a career out of blogging are ultimately the ones that are the most skilled at creating content. While some journalists and editors may lament the spread of fashion blogging, there is still a demand for strong, relevant content and currently there is still a desire among consumers to have input from fashion industry professionals. Indeed, many fashion journalists, writers, editors, designers, stylists, photographers, and visionaries are creating their own blogs and online content, in addition to the more official channels they may work with. The age of citizen journalism has arrived and there is no going back.

1 'FASHION BOY'

This illustration by Moises Quesada was inspired by influential fashion blogger Bryan Boy.

2 SUSIE BUBBLE

UK-based blogger Susanna Lau, aka Susie Bubble, has become an influential commentator on fashion and, like Bryan Boy, attends many high-profile industry events and shows.

Case study: Hall Ohara

London-born Steven Hall and Tokyo-born Yurika Ohara graduated from Central Saint Martins College, London, in 2003, and established their fashion label, Hall Ohara. They debuted their first collection during SS06 at London Fashion Week, winning the New Generation Award. The Japan-based label fully embraces digital communication, promotion, and collaboration.

The brand identity has become synonymous with precision cutting and fit. The core ethos of the label is a focus on capturing the energy of a garment, during the process of it being made. This vision led to the label being rebranded to In-Process by Hall Ohara, and the new label debuted at Japan Fashion Week AW11.

Steven Hall explains, 'We rebranded to take the line in a new direction, which has been vindicated with its development. We didn't just rebrand, we also changed the whole approach to design and pattern cutting in the studio. It was a brave choice to make, but it's worked and a few other brands out here have taken our lead, which is always a good sign.'

IN-PROCESS BY HALL OHARA

COLLECTION   ANIMATION   CONCEPT   INFO   NEWS/BLOG   WEB-SHOP

PRESS RELEASE

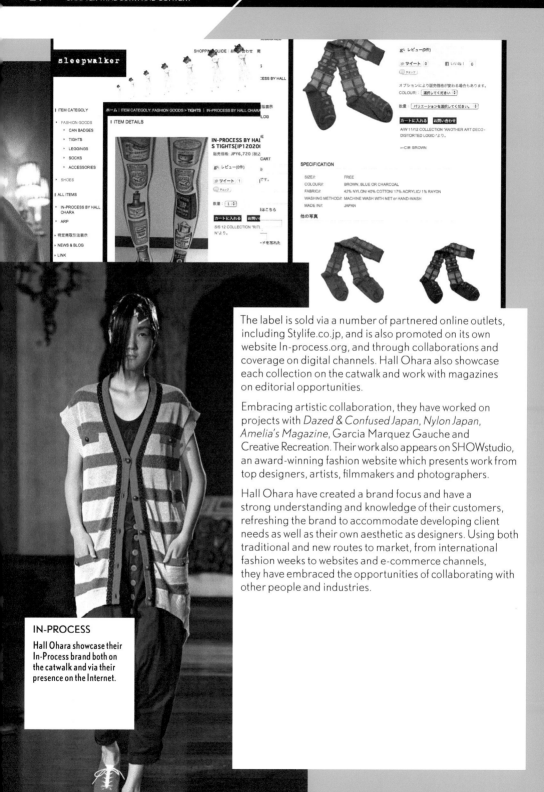

The label is sold via a number of partnered online outlets, including Stylife.co.jp, and is also promoted on its own website In-process.org, and through collaborations and coverage on digital channels. Hall Ohara also showcase each collection on the catwalk and work with magazines on editorial opportunities.

Embracing artistic collaboration, they have worked on projects with *Dazed & Confused Japan*, *Nylon Japan*, *Amelia's Magazine*, Garcia Marquez Gauche and Creative Recreation. Their work also appears on SHOWstudio, an award-winning fashion website which presents work from top designers, artists, filmmakers and photographers.

Hall Ohara have created a brand focus and have a strong understanding and knowledge of their customers, refreshing the brand to accommodate developing client needs as well as their own aesthetic as designers. Using both traditional and new routes to market, from international fashion weeks to websites and e-commerce channels, they have embraced the opportunities of collaborating with other people and industries.

IN-PROCESS

Hall Ohara showcase their In-Process brand both on the catwalk and via their presence on the Internet.

Interview: José Neves

Farfetch.com is an online-only fashion retail business. It offers customers access to stock from independent boutiques around the world. Payment to multiple boutiques, in multiple currencies, can be conducted through one process, allowing customers to buy garments from a number of retailers around the world in one transaction. José Neves is the founder of farfetch.com and has been in the fashion business for more than 20 years.

Q What led to the birth of farfetch.com?

A My other company, SIX, sells to over 300 high fashion boutiques worldwide. It struck me that they had amazing products that were relevant for the global online shopper, but very few retailers have the resources to run a top-notch e-commerce website. I thought that creating a platform for the best independent retailers would be a win-win proposition for them and provide an extraordinary experience for the consumer.

Q How did your career in the fashion industry start?

A I was born in Porto, which is a fashion industry cluster in Portugal, and my grandfather was a cobbler. I decided to launch my own shoe brand after finding out I could design shoes, so SWEAR was born in 1995. I moved to London to launch the brand internationally, and founded B Store in 2001. Although I am an economist by education, fashion fulfilled my passion for design and creative activities, and my entrepreneurial vein as well.

Q Which elements of fashion communication have impacted the way farfetch. com has developed?

A All of them. Online marketing became a very complex mix, a science and an art at the same time. You have to master all the channels to be successful; they are all important.

'I believe the future is multi-channel shopping.'

1 FARFETCH.COM

Farfetch.com offers a new way to access international, independent fashion boutiques by enabling customers to buy goods through one site and transaction.

Interview: José Neves

Q How important are up-and-coming designers to the service you offer?

A They are crucial. The whole purpose of farfetch.com is to bring an unrivalled fashion selection curated by the best independent buyers; a place where fashion enthusiasts can treasure-hunt and interact with a global fashion community, and discover new talent. The big luxury e-tailers do not stock the new talent of tomorrow, it is still the independent fashion boutique that scouts and takes risks. And these are the boutiques farfetch.com carefully selects for its marketplace, hoping to showcase those designers at the helm of fashion's creative process.

Q Do you think the media landscape has changed, in terms of how labels promote themselves to raise their profile?

A Definitely. The big media powerhouses have lost a lot of their influence. Designers are no longer made or broken by the glossy titles, 'The Devil Wears Prada' is already an anachronism.

1

Q Do you think online buying will continue to change the way we buy fashion in the future?

A Online buying is still a fraction of total retail sales. There will certainly be tremendous growth as more and more people start to buy online, and emerging markets discover and embrace e-commerce. But eventually, online sales are going to stabilize and become just another way people shop, complementary to bricks and mortar. I believe the future is multi-channel shopping.

Q Are sites like farfetch.com the way for independent boutiques to compete with the bigger brands?

A We believe so, because the capital and human resources necessary to run a successful online operation are growing relentlessly. This means that independent boutiques either need to raise funding and employ an army of e-commerce professionals, or find a shared platform that can provide them with all the tools and traffic to be able to succeed.

Q How important is it to engage with the blogger community?

A A big point of difference of farfetch.com is that we are a community. We are not an online magazine which you can shop from (a successful approach used by most other luxury sites). Instead, we are a fashion community made of boutiques, but one which also wants to engage others such as designers, bloggers, stylists, and fashion enthusiasts at large.

1   ATRIUM, NYC

Atrium is one of the high-end boutique stores represented online by farfetch.com.

Exercise: Global fashion

This exercise encourages you to consider the reasons why, and the ways in which, fashion brands adapt to various international markets.

Choose one country anywhere in the world and conduct some basic online research to identify the main fashion labels that seem to have the biggest presence there. It can be a combination of local brands and international labels, from high-street to high-end.

Look more closely at the characteristics of one of the major brands that you have identified as having a significant presence in your chosen country.

Combine the information you have discovered with some general research into the country as a whole, and see if you can come up with five reasons why you think your chosen fashion brand sells so well there.

Things to think about:

× When was the brand established? Has it got a recognized history or pedigree?
× Where does the brand's pricing sit in the market – is it considered a premium or a value brand?
× Look at the brand advertising and who it is aimed at – what is their age, lifestyle, gender?
× Look on social media sites and forums and see what you can find out about how the general public are commenting on the brand.
× How do you feel about the brand and is it targeted at you?

Compile your findings into a report on the brand, detailing your observations and how you arrived at them, including information on the research you conducted.

1 EMERGING MARKETS

Consumers crowd the famous Dongmen Pedestrian Street in Shenzhen, China.

1

Playlife

MARKETING

2

Marketing encompasses many activities and centres on the notion that, through the communication of a brand's attributes or a product's personality, consumers can be persuaded to feel a certain way about what we have to sell.

At the heart of marketing is research, which enables a level of prediction, assumption and trend forecasting. In the fast-paced fashion industry this trend forecasting is crucial for brands to be able to offer not just what the consumer wants now, but what they will want and aspire to in the future.

When it comes to satisfying the consumer, there are many ways in which to inform, entice, excite, educate and ultimately sell. This chapter looks at some of the ways in which experts predict and inform the industry, and how that process determines planned marketing strategy, as well as tactical activity.

Research and trends

Each fashion brand, large or small, will undertake some form of research before making decisions about what they want their designs to reflect and who to target them at. Many emerging designers have a personal vision of what they instinctively feel is right for them to produce, and what people will buy into. The reality, however, is that this will not always reflect what the customer is willing to pay for.

A new designer might conduct some basic research by asking people they know, as well as people they don't know, what they think of the design ideas and the brand concept. They could also scour the Internet for up-and-coming trends and predictions to help develop a potential customer profile.

It is also worthwhile to look to other industries for inspiration regarding what people are interested in, from arts and crafts, to general manufacturing techniques, music, subcultures and literature.

It can, however, be difficult to separate an emerging trend, a unique piece of research, or an original idea, from something that inspires only a few people, or is already well represented. Many designers and brands therefore rely on the services and expertise of specialist research and trend analysis companies, such as WGSN or Trendstop. These organizations conduct research for designers, as an outsourced service, on a global scale and provide analysis and predictions. These services can be invaluable for fashion brands, both large and small.

1+2 TRENDSTOP COLOUR PREDICTOR

Specialist research and trend analysis companies, such as Trendstop, offer colour prediction as one of a number of trend forecasting services.

1

2

Research and trends

1

Fashion forecasting and trend analysis

With a network of experts – creative marketing and design consultants, freelance analysts, researchers and journalists – trend forecasting organizations gather details from across the globe to help make informed predictions about what fashion consumers will turn their attention to next. Trade fairs and international trade panels also work at predicting the colours, fabrics and styling that will be favoured in the coming season. Forecasting is often carried out two years in advance of when a trend actually becomes visible to the consumer.

The information gathered by trend researchers includes details of economic and cultural developments, political influences, weather and environmental predictions, along with latest developments in interior and architectural design, as well as art, street style, and so on. Their activity is ultimately focused on gathering information about various levels of human and environmental interaction, along with cultural indicators, seasonal guidelines, historical trends and references and more, to predict what may happen next when it comes to both global and local trends.

There are also buying patterns that can be identified when it comes to researching what consumers will respond to next, and weather and seasonal changes can impact how and when people purchase. Economic patterns can be cyclical, and much of the analysis activity is based on what we know has happened in the past when certain conditions have been similar, such as during times of economic recession. So, part science and numbers, part experience and instinct, the business of fashion forecasting can be complex.

The ability of forecasting agencies to be reliable and accurate is becoming increasingly important as the market becomes more competitive and fashion seasons evolve more quickly. For designers and fashion brands, working with a fashion forecasting and trends agency to track global behavioral patterns can reduce the time they have to spend travelling and researching themselves, which can mean increased levels of productivity. The services come at a price, but for many designers they are seen as invaluable services for ensuring they have continual access to the latest developments, so that both their designs and their business remain relevant.

1 COLOUR AND FABRIC

Colour and fabric choices are among the elements that trend forecasting agencies work to predict.

TREND FORECASTING ORGANIZATIONS

Trend forecasting and research into the 'next big thing' is carried out by organizations such as WGSN, Trendstop, Promostyl, Trend Union, the International Colour Authority (ICA) which is a world leading colour forecasting service. Many brands also have their own in-house 'cool hunters', employed to go out and report on new trends and ideas, around the world. Many research companies will carry out bespoke research for a fee.

For new designers, as well as those that are very clearly focused on their own ideas and aesthetic regardless of current trends, they may be less relevant, but forecasting agencies and in-house researchers play an important role in informing the industry by reporting on what is expected to appear next.

Research and trends

Consumer behaviour and market research

To be able to devise a brand that offers something unique or mass-market, cutting edge or mainstream, it is important to have a clear understanding of what people are buying, their feelings about existing brands, and what they are likely to buy in the future.

Market research must be conducted to determine this, and can be carried out on a small scale, among contacts and acquaintances, or be outsourced to an expert research and analysis company, such as **Euromonitor International**. Companies such as this are highly skilled at conducting market research surveys and have banks of existing contacts, connections and methods of engaging with the public.

Online survey tools have also become available, some of which, such as Survey Monkey, are free. These allow a wider field of market testing, for little or no investment.

When conducting in-house research, it is important to ensure that the **consumer market research questions** used are appropriate and the target group is applicable. Possible responses offered for any multiple choice questions must enable honest answers, ensuring feedback is both relevant and useful. This is vital to be able to clearly identify how the consumer is likely to react to the brand. The larger the test group used the better, as this can provide a broader range of responses.

Market research results should enable you to begin customer profiling, which involves creating a summary of the type of customer most likely to buy your product. A customer profile describes the attributes of a potential customer, and can include demographic, geographic and psychographic (attitudes, opinions, values, etc) information, along with buying patterns, creditworthiness, and purchase history.

EUROMONITOR INTERNATIONAL

Euromonitor International is one of the many global market research organizations. It has analysts in 80 countries and conducts market research on every key trend. It provides reports on everything from socio-economic contexts to global trends and customer behaviour.

Euromonitor's research and reports can be bought, but are also available to accredited journalists for free. It is often the source of the latest industry figures quoted in the news, or statistics about the latest trend or consumer responses.

Companies of this size can be costly to engage for market research but they will often be able to tailor a survey or piece of research to suit a range of budgets.

There are a multitude of ways in which customers can be researched and profiled to aid brand development and assess market size and spending habits. Each designer or brand will develop their own ways of uncovering consumer spending patterns, loyalty, and feedback and responses to brand developments. The ongoing process of keeping in touch with what the consumer wants is imperative to brand longevity.

1

1 SHOPPING MALL

Consumer research and surveys are vital to ensure brands remain relevant and appealing to the consumer.

CONSUMER MARKET RESEARCH QUESTIONS

Basic questions you may ask prospective customers to gain an insight into their shopping habits and the market, include:

× Where do you normally shop?
× Which brands do you normally buy?
× Which brands would you like to be able to buy?
× How often do you buy fashion items?
× What is your monthly fashion budget?
× What do you read to learn about current trends?

Research and trends

JW Anderson is my homeboy. I don't know him or anything but he's Irish and therefore I can pretend to know him at dinner parties and such, to people who have no idea how big or small Ireland is. He's been tearing up the world of menswear for only a little while but he's already provided a truly unique aesthetic, a breath of fresh air if you will. With a sell out Topman collaboration under his belt he's pretty much the hottest menswear designer we have. I was unbelievably excited to see what his AW12/13 collection would look like, in his own words. It was inspired by "Aristocracy, youth culture and individualism" which left me baffled, but let's let the clothes do the talking.

Christopher Kane's AW12 show was to me a bit like a dark extension to his SS12 one. More floral motifs, more beading and embellishments, moiré instead of brocade and a palette going from blood red to bruised lips purple to black.

CHRISTOPHER KANE//

READ MORE »

categories: fashion , fashion week

THREE WAYS TO WEAR - SWEDISH HASBEENS DUCK TOE SANDALS

It's been a while since the last "Three Ways To Wear" post, but I plan on doing many more in the near future. The stars of the show right now are my new Swedish Hasbeens Duck Toe Sandals. Over the next three weeks, I will be styling them in three different ways.

Here we don't take fashion too seriously and we really like animals. If you do too, take a seat.

contact: isetta@mademoisellerobot.com

SEARCH   CONTENTS   ARCHIVE   ABOUT

search on this site

Warren is wearing: glover all coat, levi's jeans, pierre hardy sneakers and moscot glasses.

1

The influence of street style

Street style fashion has long been observed by brands and shared through channels such as the mainstream media, including TV advertising campaigns, magazine editorial and marketing programmes. 'Cool hunters' are often employed by brands to watch what's happening on the streets, ultimately helping them decide how they wish to be perceived, in terms of trend-setting. Street style blogs have had an impact on this activity and increased the accessibility of information about new trends.

The influence of contemporary fashion recorders – such as Scott Schuman – is powerful. His blog, The Sartorialist, is visited by hordes of fashion followers throughout the world, keen to see his take on what people are wearing. He photographs people whose clothes and style capture his imagination, and over time has built up a reputation as being an influential recorder of aspirational style. He collaborated with Burberry on 'The Art of the Trench' project, making use of the profile he has built as a fashion commentator to help build a loyal community for the brand, and for a particular product.

Fashion bloggers such as Bryan Boy have also influenced brands such as Marc Jacobs, who designed and named a bag after him, known as the 'BB Bag'.

So, in addition to predicting trends through traditional cultural resources and research, designers now have to keep a close eye on bloggers and street-style sites to keep up with the next generation of style influencers.

1 MADEMOISELLE ROBOT

This leading fashion blog was set up by London-based Parisian journalist Laetitia Wajnapel and covers a range of street style, personal style and observations.

2 CARDIFF CYCLE CHIC

A niche regional street style blog, looking at trends in local cycle culture.

2

Brand concept development

As we've seen, there is a need for a brand to develop a strong identity and to depict a concept, a personality, a range of attributes, an ethos and principles. Brands in the twenty-first century are expected to be multi-dimensional, and to be able to respond to external feedback and communication in a consistent and appropriate manner.

Brands can be defined in a number of ways. They can be focused on the personality at the helm of the organization, such as Julien Macdonald or Vivienne Westwood. They can represent a certain ethos or world view, such as Benetton, which depicted multiculturalism in the 1980s and 90s with provocative advertising campaigns. Diesel presents itself as the anti-fashion label, focused on original thoughts and producing advertising and ranges that echo what the creative team wants to communicate. Then there are companies like Maison Martin Margiela, which are all about a very strict brand ethos that focuses on the fashion and a collective approach to design and communication with the customer.

There are elements of a fashion brand that we, as consumers, are familiar with and that describe to us what the brand is all about – its brand concept. This is something that has to be carefully developed.

1+2 VIVIENNE WESTWOOD

Vivienne Westwood's Gold Label AW12 collection on the catwalk (1); and backstage at her AW11 show at Paris Fashion Week (2). Fashion icon Vivienne Westwood is instantly recognizable as the figurehead of her brand.

1

Brand concept development

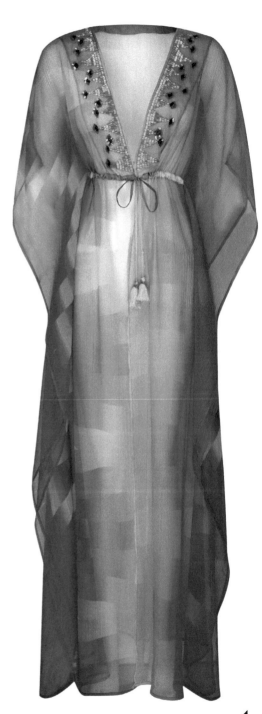

1

SWOT analysis

Before developing a brand concept, it is important to identify the key strengths and weaknesses of either the individual designer or organization. An effective way to do this is to carry out a SWOT analysis, which is a tool used across many different industries.

SWOT is an acronym of 'strengths, weaknesses, opportunities and threats'. To carry out the analysis, you write down each of the words as a heading, then a list of attributes relating to each one. For it to be truly effective, a SWOT analysis needs to be approached with honestly and clarity.

Strengths

These could be from a creative perspective or be about the financial viability of the business. For example:

×   The designer has a good reputation.
×   The business is financially stable.
×   The staff are loyal.

Weaknesses

What are the weaknesses of the designer and/or the business? For example:

×   The business has little kudos.
×   The staff have little commercial knowledge.
×   The location of the premises is not ideal.

Opportunities

These can include areas where the business could take advantage of competitor weaknesses or gain investment from new sources. For example:

×   A competitor has fallen out of favour with the media, creating an opportunity.
×   A contact is interested in a collaboration.

Threats

These could be financial, based on the industry, the environment, or competitors. For example:

×   Money in the bank is limited.
×   Creditors could withdraw funding.
×   Manufacturer prices are increasing.

Having honest answers for each part of the SWOT analysis will allow a clearer thought process when considering how to build and develop a brand story and concept. When conducting a SWOT analysis, it is also important to bear in mind market forces, consumer demands and behaviour, competitor stance and realistic opportunities for commercial development.

1   RIVER ISLAND

High-street retailer
River Island ensures all of its garments, branded items and visuals remain consistent and true to the brand's profile and principles.

Brand concept development

Defining the brand

Once information has been gathered from research, survey feedback, and SWOT analyses, opportunities can be identified and decisions made that allow a brand to be more fully developed and defined.

When developing a new brand concept, the following elements need to be considered:

- × Brand ethos – what does the brand/label stand for? What is its personality, its attitude, beliefs, aspirations, loves/hates?
- × Brand identity – what are the distinctive traits of the brand/label? What features give the brand its uniqueness and individuality? What will be the 'signature' garments/details?
- × The market – where is it? What are the market traits? How will the brand/label function in this market?
- × The competitors – who are they? These need to be identified to ensure that the brand is distinctive and superior in some way. It must have a unique selling point.
- × The customer – who are they? Where are they? Why are they the target customer? Remember, the brand cannot be everything to everyone, so it is absolutely crucial from the outset that the customer pitched at is right for the longevity and success of the brand/label.

Once these elements have been considered and decisions have been made, it is possible to incorporate them into the overall brand concept. This information can then be communicated to the target audience through marketing materials, press releases and all of the information and visuals that reflect the brand.

This process of considering the brand has to be continually revisited to ensure that the aspirations and goals originally devised are still referenced and that the market and consumer demands continue to be met.

Communicating a conscience

In developing a brand concept, it is also important to consider the brand's stance on a number of ethical issues, including those relating to materials and manufacture. Brands are increasingly required to demonstrate their principles on the human and environmental impact of what they do.

Things to consider include whether the materials used originate from a sustainable source, how much energy is used to produce the items (the carbon footprint), the working conditions of people manufacturing the garments, and whether any animal products are used.

Making statements about the sustainability of resources used is complex and requires considerable research and commitment. There are organizations that commit time and funds into investigating resources and their use, and these can give advice and also endorse a designer's commitment to the protection of resources.

1

The use of fur in fashion is an emotive subject and there have been many high-profile campaigns against it. Many designers will not use animal skins, on principle. Stella McCartney is one such designer, and has worked with animal rights charity PETA to highlight using fabrics that 'don't bleed'.

A strong stance on issues such as environmental impact, working conditions, material sourcing and animal welfare can be communicated to consumers as part of the brand identity, and will affect how they react to the brand.

The key is consistency – if a brand becomes synonymous with not using animal skins, for example, it needs to retain this stance for the life of the brand or suffer loss of brand value and customer loyalty. Statements about these issues should be factually correct and also, crucially, relate to the genuinely held beliefs of the designer.

**1 STELLA MCCARTNEY
    AW12**

The use of non-animal materials
in her collections has become a
key part of Stella McCartney's
brand identity.

Multi-channel marketing

Armed with a brand concept, a product, and market research feedback, there are a number of marketing channels to consider when building a brand profile. From print advertising and targeted email campaigns, to catwalk shows and visual merchandising, there are a variety of methods through which a brand can physically and virtually engage with and interact with the consumer.

Most brands now promote their offering through more than one channel, giving the customer the opportunity to become familiar with their attributes in a variety of ways. The key for any brand is to remain consistent, and this includes responses to customer feedback and complaints, as much as through advertising and selling.

Advertising – print and digital

Advertising in the print media is still considered an important way to connect with customers for many brands. However, as magazine circulation figures decline (according to the Audit Bureau of Circulations in the USA), many fashion brands are being forced to consider other options when it comes to engaging directly with sales channels.

Online advertising is growing in prevalence and impact and many brands are assigning significant proportions of their advertising budgets to dedicated pay-per-click digital advertising. This form of targeted advertising allows brands to decide who they want to see their adverts. The advertiser can choose to pay only for those people who clicked on their advert link. This method of advertising is not only cost-effective, but efficient in terms of connecting with the right customer. This takes advertising to a more accurate, targeted level than can be achieved in print.

1 GIANT H&M BAG

Large high-street chains such as H&M have the budgets to pay for high profile and attention-grabbing advertising stunts.

1

Many would argue, however, that digital advertising lacks the impact and shelf-life of a double-page spread in a glossy magazine, art directed, styled and photographed by industry experts. Display advertising such as this remains the domain of those who can afford it, namely luxury brands and large high-street retail chains, and magazines rely on their investment to survive. Magazines and newspapers have seen a significant decline in revenue and circulation figures in recent years, but there remains a level of demand for culturally significant and aesthetically stimulating fashion imagery for editorial and advertising in print form.

Just as with sales of goods, it is now necessary to approach advertising in a multi-channel way. A combination of targeting the right audience via focused advertising campaigns that are both offline and online (most print publications now also have an online offering), and a clear visual aesthetic, offers a culturally aware but time-strapped consumer the easiest means of responding to advertising.

Multi-channel marketing

The physical experience

Many consumers enjoy the tactile, physical experience of shopping. Retail outlets are increasingly offering consumers a number of approaches in addition to the 'physical experience', to ensure they have maximum exposure, impact and opportunities to sell. Boutiques and high-street brands vie for customer attention in new ways, and the art of visual merchandising continues to develop as an industry.

US brand Anthropologie created an in-store experience that led the shopper into a staged world of ephemeral fashion, homewares and accessories. Levi's® turned their London flagship store into 'Origin' – a whitewashed and raw-brick art and exhibition space. Many other brands have challenged our view of what a retail space is. Some newer brands, attempting to create a market presence – before investing in more permanent bricks and mortar – have invited feedback from the customer by creating elaborate experiences, through temporary 'pop-up' shops.

Although innovations such as digital changing rooms (see Fits.me, page 138) and virtual stores continue to be developed alongside mail-order and home delivery services, there still remains a strong desire for the consumer to see and feel the brands and their products in the real world.

1 SISLEY, TREVISO, ITALY

Visual merchandising is crucial in creating the desired in-store experience for consumers.

2 UNITED COLORS OF BENETTON, BARCELONA, SPAIN

Garments displayed in colour groups and merchandise priorities ensure the brand's attributes are echoed throughout the store.

1

Multi-channel marketing

1

Catwalk shows

Catwalk shows continue to be the main visual showpiece of fashion brands across the globe. They offer the most tangible depiction of what the brand offers – the garments on real people in a highly staged environment, from the theatricality of an Alexander McQueen event, to the understated elegance of Chanel and Yves Saint Laurent. Catwalk shows at recognized events, such as London, New York and Paris Fashion Weeks, are viewed as the place to see the latest in big-name new season collections, along with fledgling, cutting-edge designers.

However, catwalk shows remain out of the reach of many designers and brands, even if they gain sponsorship. For a new designer wanting to show at London Fashion Week, for example, the fee for even the most modest presence is likely to be several thousand pounds. This, in addition to the cost of producing the collection itself and any promotion carried out, before, during and after the event, can prove to be prohibitively expensive.

While some designers still embrace exclusive, invite-only atelier-style shows, others offer access to their catwalk shows online, as they happen, ensuring maximum audience exposure.

Exhibitions and trade shows that allow buyers to meet designers and view their collections in a commercial environment have also begun to appear online, enabling the viewing and buying of designs post-event. So, while the physical event may still be held regularly, there are opportunities to continue the experience online and revisit collections and designers once it is over.

What cannot be fully replicated online are the opportunities that physical events present to network with people in the same field – to share ideas and allow relationships to build and potential collaborations to flourish. This element of regular fashion industry gatherings will continue to remain important for individuals and the industry as a whole.

1 CATWALK SHOWS

Catwalk shows at fashion weeks attract significant attention from buyers, the media and the general public. They are a time-consuming and costly way to display a collection but are still strongly supported.

2 BACKSTAGE

Backstage preparations with hair and make-up artists pre-performance at a catwalk show.

2

Multi-channel marketing

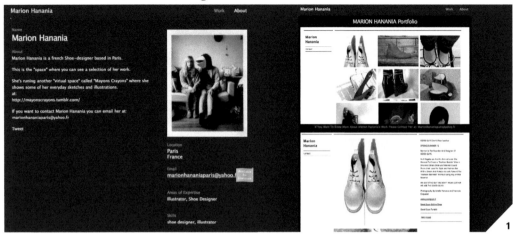

1

Collateral – branded items

Branded collateral – recorded evidence of the vision and ethos behind a brand – continues to be important when offering the customer an insight into what they can buy. As with many other elements of visual or text-based communication, much of this activity is now conducted online.

Lookbooks are often made available both in hard copy and digitally, and student portfolio sites such as Carbonmade allow collections to be showcased in a way that is free to set up and host, and easy to access. Some students still prepare hard-copy portfolios but most will now also have an online presence.

Fashion photography and the creation of visual imagery for fashion brands (discussed in more detail in chapter 4), remains a thriving industry as fashion evolves and draws on closer links with disciplines such as art, music and animation. Even though printed items have seen a decline, the desire to see a glossy, constructed view of what a clothing label can offer remains very strong. Magazines such as *Dazed & Confused* and sites such as SHOWstudio, a showpiece for conceptual fashion film, demonstrate closer links between fashion and art, and the ability to showcase the results in new and innovative ways.

1 CARBONMADE.COM

French shoe designer Marion Hanania uses Carbonmade to showcase her portfolio of work.

2

Apart from the impact digital communication has had on brand collateral, some environmentally focused campaigns, such as the reduction of retail carrier bags, effectively reduce some opportunities for the consumer to see physical branding. Once a significant opportunity for promotion, branded shopping bags may eventually become a thing of the past.

As long as there is physical participation in a fashion brand – from visiting a retail space to attending a catwalk show or visiting an exhibition – there will remain a need for printed visuals. But as print-houses continue to lose business and less of us carry business cards, in favour of smartphones that give instant access to contacts and the Internet, the need for the humble brochure or lookbook will be further called into question. The increase in information available in-store through the use of touchscreens will also reduce the need for printed materials about products and services.

2 BRANDED BAG

Branded shopping bags are
a highly visible means of
marketing on the high street.

Case study: Mary Kay pop-up store

Mary Kay Ash founded Mary Kay Cosmetics, Inc. in the US in 1963, with her life savings of $5,000 and the support of her son, Richard Rogers. Today, Mary Kay is one of the largest direct sellers of skin care and cosmetics in the world, with worldwide sales of $2.5 billion. Mary Kay products are sold in more than 35 markets worldwide, and the global independent sales force exceeds two million.

In the US, awareness of the brand has been built up over 50 years, through the legacy of Mary Kay herself, as well as television and advertising campaigns. Outside of the US, each market is encouraged to work very closely with their team of independent consultants to ensure that the brand is promoted in a way that appeals to consumers in that country.

The decision to launch a pop-up store in Cardiff, UK, in 2011 followed extensive research into the UK market, looking for areas where the brand was under-represented; both in terms of women who were likely to find the products appealing, as well as those interested in getting involved with the brand as a business.

'The public reaction to the whole concept has been incredible. We are still getting great feedback and women enquiring two months after the event about products they tried on the day and now want to purchase, or to find out more about working with Mary Kay. It is definitely a marketing method we would use in the future.'

The Cardiff pop-up store was a world first for the brand, in terms of marketing activity. The concept was chosen because they wanted an honest, genuine and fun experience for women that gave an opportunity to try the products, with professional advice and no pressure to purchase. It was about women engaging with the brand, often for the first time. The benefit of the store was that it provided the opportunity to get direct genuine feedback, wide press coverage, social media feedback and a positive, lasting association with the brand for those who visited on the day.

The very time-limited nature of this form of marketing meant that Mary Kay would directly touch around 1,000 individuals whilst the shop was open. In terms of raising brand awareness, while the number of women who were directly engaged by the brand was limited, many of the attendees spoke to their friends about their experience, enabling the positive vibe around the Mary Kay brand experience to be magnified. Press coverage reached over 750,000 readers, and press features on the store appeared around the world.

POP-UP STORE

The store allowed consumers to experience the products and talk to the company's expert consultants in a non-sales environment.

Interview: Julia Kasper

Julia Kasper is a fashion design graduate who has also
studied art. After graduating she gained valuable experience
working with designer Katie Eary, WGSN and Fashion156.com.
Currently employed as design assistant at Kanye West Ltd., she has
become a skilled fashion professional across a number of disciplines.

1 JULIA KASPER

Lookbook image from
Julia Kasper's 2011
graduate collection.

Q Was the course what you expected and did it confirm your plans to be a designer?

A Fashion design is demanding and suits a dedicated work ethos, so it's something that sat with me quite well. It allows you to be as academic as you wish through your research and reading but also gives the scope for creative freedom and a real sense of being completely self-indulgent. You can work to please yourself in design at first, only then you can focus on pleasing the client with what you have become so attached to. If it becomes your passion, then nobody can sell it better than you. I'd never planned to become an independent designer, but the course certainly equipped me with the skills and confidence to do so.

Q Why did you decide to study fashion design?

A I started off with art and design as a focus and just fell into fashion. It was the module that was most exciting to me at the time when I studied my art foundation diploma and it just became the medium with which I felt I could best express my ideas and explore creatively.

Q How important is it to have industry experience whilst you're studying?

A It's completely invaluable. You can only truly understand an industry once you've been in it. It will also aid your studies and help you to channel your strengths and home in on what you really enjoy.

Q Has your gap year experience made you more visible as a designer and helped you build contacts?

A The contacts I made on my gap year – working with international and UK-based designers – have proved integral to launching my career in the industry. It's like a snowball effect. Once you meet the first contact, who knows who you might be introduced to tomorrow?

Q What was the most valuable lesson you learned as a student about entering the fashion industry?

A Internships and experience are invaluable. It's probably said in every guide book and interview, but it's because it's just so true. You learn everything that you can't learn in a studio/classroom and make contacts that can lead to amazing things.

Interview: Julia Kasper

Q What are some of the most effective things you've done to make yourself and your work visible to your target contacts?

A Skipping the standard 'Here's my CV' email and going straight for the contacts you have made in a confident manner by telephone or email. Tell them about the most exciting thing you have been doing and who you have been working with and show genuine interest in the company or brand. Sending hyperlinks to visuals of an online portfolio makes it quick and easy for them to see what you're about, without having to download attachments and search for information.

Q How important is your online presence to you?

A Online presence is imperative in today's industry but can come across as shameless self promotion at times, so it needs to be fresh and interesting and not too gloating! I decided to set up a blog that detached itself completely from the design but carried the same aesthetic and ethos. This means personal insight, research and ideas stay separate from the online portfolio and CV. It can be a lot of upkeep, but having a few outlets for creativity online keeps your brand exciting.

Q Do digital opportunities for promotion make it easier or more difficult for young designers to stand out from the crowd?

A I guess with so many blogs, portfolios and sites it's even more difficult to stand out in the online sector. The juxtaposition of online, print, events or other media is obviously going to be more exciting than the average student blog. It just needs to be thought out and justified, and if the design is good, of course you can stand out.

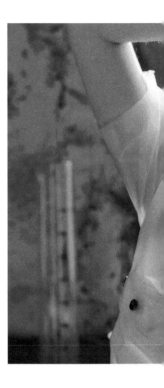

1

1 BRAND ETHOS

Julia's brand focuses on a strong
design ethos and developed
brand 'story'.

Q What else do you plan on
doing to promote the 'Julia
Kasper' brand, whether that
be as a designer, forecaster
or stylist?

A I'm freelancing as a
pattern cutter at the
moment but I'm keen to
work in whatever medium
becomes available and is
interesting at a given time.
I'm trying to keep up with
the blog while I freelance
full-time and continue
contributing as a writer to
other sites. It's important
to keep your name out
there but it can be difficult
to prioritize that when you
are concentrating on doing
your job to the best of your
ability. At the moment I'm
concentrating on doing my
freelance pattern cutting
to the best standard I can,
and nurturing existing
and new relationships with
the contacts I'm meeting
through this job.

Q What do you think is the
most valuable promotional
tool for a designer?

A Collaborations. Meeting
like-minded people with
the vision and skills that you
need to promote your work.
Photographers, filmmakers,
stylists, writers, hair and
make-up artists... you can't
do it all alone! You can try,
but it's a lot easier and a lot
more fun doing it through
creative collaboration.

Q How would you like your
career to progress?

A At some point, I'd love
to be in the position to
set up the label and do a
collection. You don't realize
it at the time, but doing your
graduate collection is so
self-indulgent and can be so
self-fulfilling if you let your
creativity run wild. It's not
often that you'll get to do
that when you're working for
someone else or for a client.
So getting to a stage when
I can create and design for
myself, having a completely
singular vision and outcome;
that would be amazing.

*'If it becomes your passion, then nobody
can sell it better than you.'*

Exercise: Creating a brand concept

This exercise looks at how to approach creating a fashion brand concept from an original idea. If you were thinking about setting up a label, consider the main reasons why you would want to design clothes, shoes or accessories. What makes you passionate about expressing your creativity?

Conduct an honest SWOT analysis about you and what you have to offer as a designer. Referring to the guidelines on page 49, consider what to include in a list of your:

× Strengths
× Weaknesses
× Opportunities
× Threats

Once you've identified what you have to offer as well as any limitations, think about what matters to you most as a designer. Is it that you want to produce garments that only make use of natural materials? Do you want to be a cutting-edge designer focused on creating something truly unique, or do you want to create highly wearable, functional, but beautiful everyday fashion?

Next, think about what you and your brand will stand for – your identity, the market you want to sell in and who your customers might be. Making these decisions early on will enable you to be focused and clear about other decisions you will have to make at different stages of your brand's development.

1 ELLY SNOW

Elly Snow's striking collection Machinery and Manipulation explored ideas of the battle between man and nature, through the juxtaposition of strong fabrics and organic sculptural forms.

1

MEDIA AND PR

3

The media as a whole has experienced considerable change and evolution in recent times. The explosion of citizen journalism and blogging has meant that the fashion media has experienced some of the biggest changes of all. The fashion consumer can now as easily read and be inspired by blogs as magazines.

The impact this has had on traditional fashion media has been complex and significant. Good content, however, is still key, and well-written, timely and factually correct independent journalism is still regarded the most highly. But how do we differentiate between good and bad writing, and those that write from experience, compared to the rest? As the media landscape has become busier, and opportunities for coverage have increased, those wishing to appear in print have to be more discerning about where they want to be seen.

1 RED CARPET EVENTS

Penélope Cruz wearing L'Wren Scott at a film premiere. Having a high-profile celebrity wear your brand can generate huge media and consumer interest.

Fashion PR

Fashion public relations (PR) has developed into a fast-paced and competitive industry that attracts large numbers of eager interns and graduates each year. For many of those interested in fashion PR careers, getting unpaid agency or in-house experience is a valuable foot in the door to an industry that is perceived as both glamorous and exciting. The reality can be glamorous, but it is also a demanding occupation that is often less well paid than similarly graded PR roles in other industries.

Public relations, in its purest form, is about establishing and managing relationships with all of the 'publics', or audiences, that an organization comes into contact with. PR is often defined as press or media activity, but it can also encompass how companies communicate with many other types of people. It includes working with the media, but also the general public, online audiences, employees, suppliers, buyers and others.

Fashion PR is primarily focused on gaining press and media coverage for designer collections, but can also include working directly with buyers to encourage them to view and buy collections, networking with industry contacts, managing catwalk shows, press days, establishing relationships between designers and potential collaborators, and much more.

FASHION PR CAREERS

Renowned for offering glimpses of a glamorous industry and the potential to rub shoulders with celebrities, fashion PR has become one of the most challenging sectors to gain entry to, for both interns and job applicants.

If you're interested in getting experience with a fashion PR agency, look out for their annual internship schemes, but be prepared to face tough competition.

To work in fashion PR, you will need excellent communication skills, the ability to event manage, organize and be able to multi-task, and the confidence to pitch and present ideas, concepts and collections to a variety of audiences.

1 FASHION PRESS

Anna Wintour, editor-in-chief of US *Vogue* magazine, attends the runway for a collection by Derek Lam at Mercedes-Benz New York Fashion Week in 2011.

Fashion PR

In-house or outsourced?

Some fashion designers and brands work with external PR agencies, while others employ in-house staff. Working with an agency has the advantage of giving instant access to a vast array of established industry and media contacts, that a designer would take years to build up on their own. A good PR agency will also know how to create information about brands and how to pitch it to the right people.

The growth of online communication has presented increased opportunities for fashion brands, large and small, to carry out elements of PR activity themselves. By researching the most influential online magazines, blogs, social media commentators, reviewers and writers, it is possible to start building direct relationships with them through email, blogging and posting online.

Many designers, for both cost and control reasons, combine outsourced PR agency help with conducting a number of activities themselves. A PR agency can be engaged, for example, to focus on writing and distributing press releases, organizing and running press days, and making use of their valuable contacts to alert media and buyers to designer collections. A designer can then supplement this activity by running their own social media profiles, communicating with bloggers and industry contacts online and communicating on a more personal level among industry network groups.

Finding an agency that fits

There are a number of factors to take into account when deciding which agency is right for you. These include **agency costs**, location, expectations and perhaps even their principles about fashion, production and communication techniques. A good agency will be upfront and realistic about what they can and can't achieve for a designer, and will be able to make informed decisions about the most effective and relevant media and contacts for a particular brand to engage with.

1

It is important to be clear at the outset of a relationship with a PR agency what your objectives are, how the results will be measured, and also what the main factors for campaign success are.

The type of agency is also an important consideration, and whether or not their existing client list complements a new designer. If an agency has an impressive list of high-end, well-known brands, a fledgling designer may find they don't receive the attention expected because their budget doesn't operate at the same level as the rest of the agency's clients. Small 'boutique' agencies often seek out new designers as they can make their name on being a proactive consultancy that uncovers new, raw talent, and spends time and effort on nurturing industry relationships for small fashion businesses.

Ultimately, it is important to conduct research, speak to as many people with relevant experience as possible, and visit and speak to the agencies themselves, before deciding to work with one. The agency should be able to demonstrate their understanding and passion about your work, so that they can communicate this to your target audience.

1 PR AGENCY
CATALOGUE

Pages from Bloody Gray PR's
press day book, with profile
details, images and news about
the brands they represented.

AGENCY COSTS

In terms of costs and invoicing, there are three main ways in which PR agencies tend to work:

- × Retained fee basis – this means they charge an agreed monthly amount for a certain number of hours or days of work, and agree upfront what activities will be carried out.
- × Project basis – this means they only charge for completing an agreed number of activities, for example, introduction to two buyers and one feature in a magazine.
- × Results basis – this means they will only invoice once they have secured a desired result, such as securing an editorial feature, for example.

Fashion PR

Press days

Press days are a key activity in the fashion industry calendar. They are held by the majority of fashion PR agencies and larger fashion brands to enable the media and buyers to see the latest collections up close, and to assess whether to feature them, use the garments in photoshoots, or place orders. The challenge for many brands today is that press days are run throughout the year and many journalists and buyers have to be highly selective about which they attend, as they are invited to so many.

Press days can be held at a PR agency's offices, a location such as a hotel, or in-house at the designer's studio. In the UK, the majority are held in London as this is where the main fashion press and buyers are based and, with the competition evident, it is important to make it as easy as possible for guests to attend.

Press packs and lookbooks are generally made available at these events, which give the opportunity to directly engage with key industry influencers. Press packs should contain a designer biography and brand background, a collection lookbook, details of where the collection is stocked, as well as full contact details.

A well-organized and attended press day can offer a designer an excellent opportunity to put their collection in front of interested and influential media and buyers.

1

1 LIBERTY LONDON PRESS DAY

Press days such as this allow the fashion press to see a brand's latest collections in one place.

Working with celebrities

Modern consumers continue to watch celebrities avidly – as soon as a new look is seen on the red carpet at a film premiere, it is shared worldwide on websites and blogs. For a designer, having garments from their latest collection worn by a celebrity that regularly appears in the public eye can have a significant impact on sales. As consumer aspirations to emulate a celebrity lifestyle continue to grow, and reality TV continues to expand, celebrity endorsements have an even bigger impact.

For designers it is important to consider which celebrities they would like to be seen wearing their garments, and how that celebrity embraces what the brand stands for. This is a good starting point for making decisions about which famous people to offer garments to. A PR agency will have relationships with some celebrities and if a designer wants items to be sent to a particular celebrity, will have an understanding of how best to approach this.

2 **FASHION PRESS WEEK**

Fashion Press Week gives
members of the fashion
press the opportunity to see
new collections from several
designers in one place
(see page 86).

2

Approaching people that we see on our
television and movie screens every day can
be a daunting task, but if a celebrity feels an
affinity with a brand, they are often happy to
be seen supporting the label. A great shot of
a high-profile celebrity in a key look from a
designer's collection can be enough PR for
some brands to last a long time.

Building media relations

Building connections with the media takes time, commitment and a clear understanding of the readership of each publication you approach.

Journalists will only be interested in material that is relevant to their readers, whether that be for a newspaper, glossy magazine or blog. Without readers, a publication loses the ability to create revenue through advertisers, who look for reader numbers. Even for bloggers, without an audience the impetus to share thoughts and information with others would quickly be lost.

Working with a fashion PR agency that has existing connections and contacts can provide the perfect way for many designers to build connections with the media, giving them exposure that would otherwise be difficult to obtain. This can, however, be too costly for many fledgling fashion businesses.

If working directly with journalists, it is important to remember that they like to be kept informed on a regular basis of what's happening, sometimes expecting exclusives and information in advance of general release, so they can beat their competition to a new story.

Bloggers have different pressures to journalists and their deadlines may be created for entirely different reasons. A number of bloggers work from home and may have to balance family commitments with a full-time job, so they may only work on their blogs in the evenings. They do, however, play an increasingly important role in communicating news so it is important to ensure that you consider bloggers when building your media contacts.

1+2   *VOGUE* IPAD APP

The print version of glossy magazine *Vogue* is now complemented by a digital iPad app. Whatever format of fashion media you target, an understanding of its readership is crucial.

Building media relations

Understanding the reader

While it is ultimately the journalist or writer's responsibility to understand the needs and preferences of their readers, anyone wanting the media to write about them must also have a strong understanding of the sort of news and information that is of interest and that sells.

If you want to be covered by *Vogue*, for example, you will need a very clear understanding of who reads it and what they expect from it. Even if you think you know who the readers of a publication are, you should check the profile of the publication by accessing its **advertising information data**, which is usually available online. This is intended to demonstrate to advertisers the audience demographic for a publication, highlighting the type of reader their adverts would need to be targeted at.

Ultimately, the best way to assess what the reader is looking for from a particular publication is to read it yourself. To get a feel for what the reader wants and expects, you only have to take a look at the images, the editorial, regular features and advertisers. As you read through relevant magazines to assess their readership, it is also worth familiarizing yourself with the regular sections and columns, as these can provide good opportunities for you to supply timely and relevant information that works within an existing format. Understanding a publication and how it covers topics and news, and then making informed and relevant suggestions for input, can be much more powerful than sending a general press release to the editor.

Likewise with bloggers, the only way to get a clear understanding of what their readers are looking for is to read their blog, including its archived articles, comments and social media profiles linked to the blog. Facebook and Twitter can be powerful communities and forums, where conversations are held that give a real insight into what interests blog readers.

ADVERTISING INFORMATION DATA

To find the advertising information data for a publication, you need to find out who the publisher is. IPC Media is the publisher of *Marie Claire*, for example. The advertising information data for *Marie Claire* is available on the IPC Media website – www.ipcadvertising.com/ipc-brands. Further details can be obtained by requesting a media or advertising pack. The *Marie Claire* reader is described as an ABC1 professional woman, aged between 25–34. The ABC1 listing is a demographic classification based on occupation. ABC1 spans the upper- to lower-middle classes with occupations ranging from higher managerial to administrative or clerical.

1 *VOGUE ITALIA*

Iconic fashion magazine *Vogue* has several international editions and remains a prestigious publication.

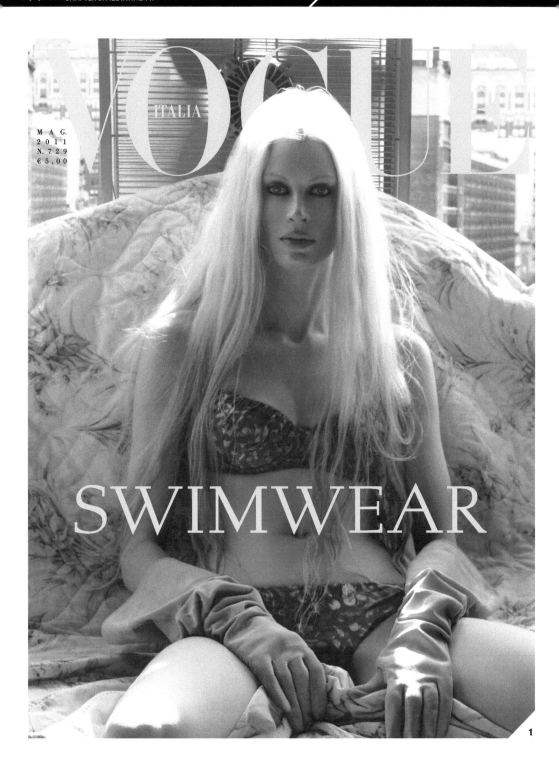

Building media relations

Creating a media target list

Armed with background information, an understanding of the reader, a list of applicable columns and features and knowledge of what's been covered before, a media target list can be built.

As with most data sources, building a useful and current media target list takes time and patience and a considerable amount of research. It's a good idea to begin with a larger list of all of the magazines, newspapers, blogs and broadcast contacts that you would like to print your news and information and then edit it down into a smaller list of priorities. Include a top tier of approximately ten key contacts that represent the most desirable publications you would like to cover your stories.

MEDIA TARGET LISTS

A comprehensive media target list should include the following information:
× Publication name.
× Brief description – e.g. women's lifestyle magazine.
× Publication type – print or digital?
× Frequency – how often is it published?
× Readership – the numbers that read each edition. Some publications have an officially recognized readership number, others have their own validation of reader numbers, so be aware of this.
× Contact name – this could be the editor if it's a small publication, or for larger publications it will need to be a specific contact, such as the fashion editor.
× Preferred method of contact – it is preferable to have email and telephone contact details, so you can follow up an email with a phone call. Some journalists will only accept submissions via email, however.

1

There are a number of media list subscription services available that allow access to a researched and up-to-date database of contacts for a monthly fee. These can be refined to build your own tailored list. They can be costly to subscribe to, but save a lot of time. Fashion Monitor, Mediadisk and ResponseSource are just some of these services. Most PR agencies subscribe to a list of this sort that can be refined for each client.

There are also press release or newswire distribution services and news syndication services that charge a fee for sending out text and/or images to a large database of contacts. This is more of a scattergun approach that can gather coverage across a much broader range of publications, especially online. Examples of these include PR Newswire and SourceWire.

A number of the publications that cover stories using this method can be obscure, but a presence across a number of online sites can boost search engine optimization (SEO) presence and numbers, which can also help raise brand awareness (see pages 110–111).

2

1 MAGAZINE STAND

With the vast number of publications available, it is vital to target those most relevant to your brand.

2 GRAZIA

Glossy fashion and beauty magazine, GRAZIA, is published weekly, allowing it to cover fashion news and trends more frequently than its monthly counterparts.

Creating content for distribution

Creating content such as features, press releases, news alerts and product details forms the basis of a significant amount of PR activity. This can be challenging and time consuming if a target publication's content and preferences are not clearly understood. Some publications issue editorial guidelines with details of how they prefer to receive submissions. Some also provide editorial team contact details and information about which areas each journalist covers. This should provide a clear indication of what the publishers are looking for.

Most publications also issue guidelines on submitting images to accompany a press release or feature. These will refer to the image format, caption and other information regarding image copyright, the file size and also the style of the image. It is vital to study the type of images and 'feel' of the visual aspects of a publication to gain a full understanding of what they are likely to accept and, ultimately, print.

While most publications will accept press releases – generally in digital format – not all will be receptive to lengthier features or ideas for them. Some will, however, accept a brief summary of a suggested feature, in a couple of paragraphs. If they consider it will fit in with the publication, they may then ask for the article to be submitted in full.

1   THE BUSINESS OF FASHION

This renowned digital magazine founded by Imran Amed has gained a huge following based on its authoritative, well-written content.

Bloggers and other digital content writers will often accept contributed content, and may allow and openly encourage contributed guest blog posts, images, features and product updates.

The three most important considerations when working with the media are to know and understand the publication targeted, understand their audience, and to never contact them on deadline day!

Press releases

Press or news releases are the most common method of communication for many designers, PR agencies and in-house press teams. A press release offers a journalist or writer information that will be concise, topical, and based on factual details that are of interest to their readers. **Press release content** is generally geared at releasing news and information that hasn't previously been available and is relevant at the time of release. There is no point in sending out details of an event or launch that has either already happened (unless offering a review of a successful event), or is going to happen a long time in the future.

5 April, 2012 | by BoF Team

)aily Digest | Waiting for China's moment, rest's path, The Gap and teens, Future of retail, Nail boom

Yau Meiyue Spring/Summer 2012 | Source: Fashion Inquisitive

e China Fashion Week era arrive? *(China Daily)*

eks are being staged everywhere,and there's practically a host city for every lett ntly hosted China Fashion Week, which got some media mileage overseas, but an the agenda of the global fashion industry's movers and shakers."

going to make any money? *(Telegraph)*

nterest and a range of social curation sites that enable us to search for and pin ages to virtual boards, and then share them. Eventually Pinterest will have to ?, but it will have to be from browsers, not buyers, because Pinterest won't cant purchasing."

ore teens ringing the register *(Market Register)*

Inc.'s target demographic may be those ages 25 to 40, the largest U.S. clothing nd up benefiting disproportionately from a recovery in teen apparel

ndi's Asleug Magnusdóttir On the Future of Online Retail *(Fashionetc)*

nuing to enhance the technology. That's really important for us. We are looking video, we're looking at making this experience of shopping even more han it has been. We will continue to broaden the selection. We'll introduce shop, so you can shop more by trend, and shop the editorials."

g as Polishes Boom *(NY Times)*

onths, cosmetics makers have invested in lacquers a kind of daring all but decade ago, introducing innovations from glitter and crackled surface

.rchive

1

Creating content for distribution

Biography and profile

To gain further understanding of news and other information sent out from a brand, journalists are often interested in the people behind the brand. Information of interest is likely to include where they come from, what their experience is, what they have done in the past, along with some relevant personal details. Creating a professional biography to address this is important as it encourages a connection with brand customers, as people increasingly look for the human element of what they are buying into. Ensuring this information is readily available online on branded websites and social media profiles is also important for brand connection and consistency.

Consider designers such as Vivienne Westwood and Tom Ford, for example, whose personal profiles, beliefs, and experience are integral to their brand and what it stands for. Not all designers approach the public face of their brand in this way, but for new designers, creating a personal element to the brand can lead to a closer understanding of the customer. Professional photographs can also be provided to depict the people behind the brand, which the reader will become familiar with and recognize over time.

Features and other formats

Features and lengthier, more involved opportunities to contribute to magazines, newspapers and broadcast channels can also be secured, giving an opportunity to provide more column inches in targeted publications. These can take the form of an in-depth interview with a designer, a feature on an industry issue that may include contributions from other designers, or a comment piece on a particular trend or style. The possibilities are seemingly endless, and many publications are open to ideas for features if they are presented in an informed and concise manner and demonstrate a sound knowledge of the publication itself.

PR agencies are adept at 'pitching in' ideas for features and at the placement of stories with targeted publications. For designers approaching this independently, building strong relationships with journalists over time by consistently offering up information in a relevant and timely manner can create opportunities for story and feature ideas in the future.

1

Ania Maria Rozanowska   Work   About

Name
Ania Maria Różanowska

About
Ania Maria Różanowska

Ania Maria Różanowska is a Polish born fashion designer educated in
Wales and Finland. Working for an innovative footwear designer Chau Har
Lee and a luxury furniture brand Jimmie Martin in London has given her
an insight into different design fields.
The AMR philosophy is to design and manufacture timeless collections of
garments and accessories, where the key to each piece is the exploration
of delicate movement, structural shape and feminine transparency
through high quality materials, beautiful finishes and skilled
craftsmanship.

Dimension of Infinity

The collection explores the infinity of time and the three dimensional
structure. The beauty of form follows the principles of symmetry,
avoiding random miss matching, yet still managing to capture movement
within each garment. There is an obvious presence of white, evoking
purification of thoughts and inviting the mind to fantasise. Each garment
from the collection has been handcrafted to the highest standard in fine
silks and bespoke platinum dipped skins. AMR accessories were
developed in collaboration with Industry partners and experiment with
the intimate relationship between the material and the manner in which it
channels light, producing effects that cannot be repeated and that look
different at any moment and angle.

Awards

Dimension of Infinity collection has won an award for 'Collection of the
Year 2011'.
'Best of Welsh Graduate Design Awards 2011' Winner

Location
United Kingdom

Email
rozanowska@gmail.com

Areas of Expertise
Winner of 'Collection of the Year 2011'
Award

Skills
Research, Fabric Sourcing, Pattern
Cutting, Adobe Photoshop

2

Maintaining your profile

Once relationships have been developed
with the media, whether via a PR agency or
directly, it is important to ensure that these
contacts are kept informed of label and
collection updates and developments on a
regular basis. Media interest in the brand
should be maintained by ensuring they are
communicated with and perhaps offered
exclusive information.

If a journalist makes a request for further
details or images, they should be responded
to immediately – if they are not, they may
look elsewhere for information and images
from another designer.

Keeping websites and social media
channels up to date and creating content
on own-branded blogs is also important
as it shows evidence of a committed and
informative communicator and allows
interested parties to be kept informed about
the label.

Maintaining a consistent and regularly
updated profile across key channels is
much more involved than simply sending
out a press release at the launch of each
new collection. This is a consideration
when deciding whether or not to invest in
outsourced media and PR assistance.

1+2   ANIA MARIA RÓZANOWSKA

Fashion graduate Ania showcases her
AMR brand and has a strong biography
and profile on her branded website,
rozanowska.carbonmade.com.

Case study: Fashion Press Week

Established by PR consultant Sam Fearn, Fashion Press Week was launched at the Saatchi Gallery in London in November 2010. Sam Fearn has worked in PR for more than ten years and began her career with Weber Shandwick PR in New York after graduating from Leeds University. She was headhunted by Hill and Knowlton PR in New York, before returning to the UK in 2001.

Sam established her agency, Fearnhurst PR, in London and currently works with a number of well-known high-street brands including AllSaints, Hobbs, Pied a Terre, Nine West, Bertie, Kenneth Cole, Kookai and Pandora. Familiar with press days herself and the time and costs involved in managing and hosting them, she decided to look for an alternative approach.

FASHION PRESS WEEK

Selected members of the fashion press have the opportunity to view a broad range of new labels in one place, at one time.

'The first three events have indicated that this is a formula that the industry was ready for and works for a large number of designers, agencies, and the media.'

Sam explains, 'The media get invited to numerous press days throughout the year. For many journalists, stylists and photographers interested in seeing garments and meeting designers but short on time, they are a necessary luxury. I decided to find a way to bring together designers, their PR representatives and the media in one location twice a year, to see if the whole process could be made more efficient.'

Exhibitors are chosen by a panel of industry experts. They are selected as part of a representative cross-section of brands and retailers and include emerging designers, ethical brands, high-street brands, accessory companies, wholesalers, department stores, childrenswear designers, and international brands.

Collaborative events of this nature are being seen more often across the industry, as people become more focused on efficiency and are challenged by time constraints. The benefit for brands, the press and buyers is that everyone can capitalize on multiple opportunities and exposure at one event, in one location, at one time.

Interview: Rebecca Gray

Bloody Gray PR is a boutique fashion PR agency that represents rising as well as established design stars across the industry. Founded in 2010, Bloody Gray has built up a reputation of being a supportive and nurturing agency that works with clients it connects with and truly believes in. Rebecca Gray is its founder and MD.

1

Q How was Bloody Gray PR set up and why?

A We've been established for almost two years now, although my experience in PR has spanned a much longer period and I've previously run my own agency in Australia. After working in London for a while I was initially approached by a couple of designers I knew who weren't happy with the service they were getting from their agencies and encouraged me to start my own consultancy. As we've delivered results for clients and not charged the earth for doing it, the business has grown organically through word-of-mouth. It is important for me to love what I do, and to represent clients I understand and believe in.

Q How do you work with clients?

A Some work with us on a monthly fee retainer, some are project-based and others pay on results. When you're working with new and emerging designers you have to be flexible and you also have to help them to solidify their offering and the way they work, to enable them to be more sustainable for the long-term. We are always interested in the designer and us being the right fit for each other, and looking at where we can take the label in the future.

Q Who is a typical Bloody Gray client?

A They have to be emerging and something that hasn't been seen before; unique. They have to be able to grow in the industry, have a dynamic approach and need to be open to gaining a clearer understanding of the industry, if they don't have that awareness or knowledge already.

1 PRESS DAY

Collections on display at the
Bloody Gray PR press day.

Interview: Rebecca Gray

Q **What are the challenges new designers must face to raise their profile?**

A There are many challenges facing new designers. Lack of experience and financial support are probably the most difficult to overcome at the outset, combined with lack of contacts or an industry network of experts and collaborators. It is also becoming harder to get press coverage in magazines as there is increased competition. A new business also has to build a list of stockists and sales routes, so that when they do appear in publications, people know where they can purchase the garments.

Q **How important are press days in fashion PR?**

A They generally work better for larger companies. In my case, as a smaller firm, they are important in terms of branding and raising product awareness within the industry. All of my designers showcase during fashion week, which means the industry has already seen the products. More than anything, press days are a great opportunity for networking, branding and general exposure. A long-term strategy and long-term media planning needs to support this sort of activity.

Q **How important is celebrity endorsement in fashion PR?**

A It is hugely important, especially in the UK. Case studies prove it too. Cheryl Cole, for example, exposed designer David Koma to mainstream attention, and anytime a celebrity wears one of my designers' pieces on the red carpet we are inundated with enquiries.

'To raise your profile you need to explore the bigger picture and look at collaborations, cruise collections, corporate projects...'

Q How have built up your press/buyer/stylist contacts list?

A Lots of personal hard work, hitting the phones, researching and emailing people. I've also used some of the online media list services such as Fashion Monitor and Diary Directory.

Q What advice would you give a new designer looking for a PR agency?

A Make sure you don't get lost among all of the other designers represented by the agency. An agency needs to make money but don't let that be at your expense. Make sure you have a friendly and strong relationship with your account handler and that you are in constant contact with them to ensure the job is being done.

Q Any tips on creating content to raise your profile?

A Anyone can design and make clothes. To raise your profile you need to explore the bigger picture and look at collaborations, cruise collections, corporate projects and how you can share the details of all of the entrepreneurial things you do, with the right audiences.

Q Do you work with interns?

A We are regularly contacted by interns. It's a great learning experience to be an intern, however it does depend on the company and the responsibilities and activities the intern takes part in. Sometimes, interning with a smaller company is better as you can really make a difference to the success of the company. On the flip side, if you have valuable skills and work extremely hard it is likely that this will be noticed and the potential for employment can be greater at a larger company. It also depends on the individual's confidence, skill set and work ethic.

Exercise: Creating brand content

Using the five Ws principles (see page 83) of writing a press release about a collection, create a brief news release, two or three paragraphs in length. It could focus on either your own or another brand, and should be written with relevant target media in mind.

Think about the most important element of the story, and what would be most compelling to the target readers. If you're releasing a new collection but it's not your first, think about what makes the second collection different, and the reasons for the new approach. If the collection is similar to a previous one, think about why – was this a response to positive customer feedback?

Journalists receive dozens of releases a day, so yours has to offer something interesting and memorable in order to stand out. If you're a very young designer or you have transferred from another industry, that could be what's unique about you. Alternatively, it could be that you've collaborated with others to produce the collection, or that the materials you've used are unusual.

Ask others what they think is your brand's unique selling point (USP), as they can take a more objective view. Ask friends and family, colleagues and customers what they think makes each collection stand out and work this information into your press release.

Try to keep your release brief, to the point and make sure it includes all the relevant details, such as where an event is happening or a collection is being launched, how people can obtain further details and contact you, and where potential customers can buy your collection.

1 STUDENT SHOW

Your release could be about promoting a student collection, or the results of a student fashion competition, such as this one in Bangkok, Thailand.

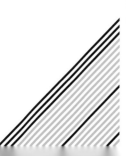

1

CREATING THE VISION

4

The fashion industry is driven by the visual; concepts, styling and the presentation of a subjective aesthetic. This is clear when looking at the imagery presented by magazines and by the brands themselves. Without this visual representation, creative editing and styling, looks and trends become just clothes.

The fashion industry capitalizes on our desire to say something about ourselves through the way we dress. All brands carefully shape and develop the visual representation of their products in order to make customers feel a particular way. The fashion industry is built on painting a desirable picture for the consumer.

There are many ways for a brand to create and communicate their vision with the consumer; this chapter will look at some of the most common tools and techniques available.

1 POPPY ROBERTS

Poppy produces distinct
fashion-based illustrations
that depict a strong style and
personality (see case study on
page 114).

Photography and styling

Fashion magazines *Vogue* and *Harper's Bazaar* pioneered the notion of stylized fashion photography, and in the 1920s and 1930s they employed in-house fashion photographers, including the likes of Cecil Beaton. These played a key role in transforming the genre into an art form. More recent photographers such as Patrick Demarchelier, Mario Testino, Annie Leibovitz, and Rankin have all continued this tradition and produced some of the most inspiring images of the twentieth and twenty-first centuries.

Today, fashion photography of styled models, scenes, props and accessories is used for advertisements, editorial features in fashion magazines, campaigns and online.

A very different type of fashion photography that has become essential to designers is known as 'still life fashion'. This is photography of the garments alone, without models. These are taken for display, to inform the consumer about the product and its attributes, with very limited styling. It is now an important part of fashion retailer marketing and e-commerce offerings.

1 STYLED FASHION IMAGE

Part of fashion design student Alyyson Arscott's 2011 collection, this photograph was taken by fashion photographer Ali Johnson.

Working with fashion photographers

Fashion photographers come in all abilities and charge varying amounts of money, depending on their skills and experience. It is best to work with the most experienced photographer that your budget will allow.

Some photographers need to schedule photoshoots weeks in advance, while others can be booked at short notice. It is useful to look at their previous work and to find out how they prefer to work. Do they welcome input from the designer, or are they reluctant to receive direction? Some designers are happy to supply garments, models and props, and leave the styling and photography to the professionals. A certain amount of trust has to be gained before most designers will allow photographers *carte blanche* on a photoshoot.

2 STILL LIFE FASHION

In contrast to the image opposite, still life photographs such as this show the product alone, without any styling.

PHOTOSHOOT CONSIDERATIONS

It is important to establish how each professional on a photoshoot will work, and who will be responsible for what. Ask yourself the following questions:

× What will the photographer arrange? A studio, props, models – or is the designer expected to do this?
× What will the designer arrange – models, make-up and hair, facilities for the models to get ready, refreshments?
× Has permission been arranged with the owner of the location?
× Is the charge per hour, or per photo session?
× Are expenses to be charged for travel and meals?
× How will the images be supplied following the shoot?
× Who has ultimate copyright of the images and control over how they can be used?

A considerable amount of pre-planning and organization is required to ensure a photoshoot is conducted efficiently and that it will yield the most positive results.

1

Photography and styling

Art direction – communicating the vision

Having a clear understanding of the vision you want the photography to convey is key to both the brand and the collection.

Many designers will approach a photoshoot with a character or story in mind. Some designers approaching a photoshoot may look back to the inspiration behind the designs and aim to incorporate elements of that into the images. Others will retain that inspiration throughout the development of the collection, and the photoshoot will be a continuation of the story being created as the garments evolve.

Whichever approach is taken, the inspiration will be depicted through the garments, styling, models, location, props and accessories. This inspiration will need to be clearly communicated to all professionals involved, either via a combination of written details and moodboards, or verbal direction on the day of the shoot. Stylists and hair and make-up artists will need clear direction regarding what look is to be created.

The selection of models, hair and make-up artists, location and props is vital to ensure that the right aesthetic for the brand and the garments is depicted. Choosing models can be a daunting task, but before arranging a casting it is a good idea to make a list of the attributes the ideal model would have. Unlimited budgets allow access to a large number of models and hair and make-up stylists, but when funds are limited, universities and colleges are often a great place to find enthusiastic and creative people studying relevant subjects.

Props and background elements that are to be included in the styling of the shoot can be sourced from film studios, vintage shops, professional prop hire companies, personal belongings, and so on.

A successful photoshoot is arrived at through a combination of good planning and organization, a clear understanding of the desired end visuals, flexibility, clear communication, some inspiration and a little risk-taking on the day!

1 **CREATING THE LOOK**

Hair and make-up artists will require clear guidance on what look the designer wants to create.

1

2

2 SHELLEY JONES

Shelley Jones is a fashion
photographer with a keen eye
for depicting a visual 'story'
through her images, evidenced
in this striking self-portrait.

Photography and styling

1

Styling

A growing and significant part of the fashion industry, fashion styling has become an art form in itself, with many of the most reputable stylists in high demand by designers, brands and photographers. No longer confined to creating simplistic images of garments and collections, styling can be used to convey complex concepts that suggest narratives about a brand and its underlying personality.

Styling can range in creativity from straightforward catalogue or online shoots, to conceptual magazine editorial that evokes much more about a brand than simply the clothes. All fashion photography incorporates some elements of styling and editing, but the range of creative input can vary greatly.

Many stylists work as freelancers, making their services available to designers, brands, magazines and other publications, as well as to film and video production companies. Others are employed in-house. Good stylists will respond to a client's brief while also offering something of their own individual talent and creativity.

Sourcing the services of a good stylist is the same as looking for any professional service where creativity is involved. It is important to see examples of their work and to get feedback from previous clients, to get a sense of how a stylist works. Their creative focus and how they approach a project is equally important. For a designer, a stylist's ability to see the vision as they do and bring their own creative ideas to the table can be more important than their credentials.

1+2 MICHELLE VICTORIA McGRATH

Designer Michelle McGrath works closely with photographers to present a strong visual identity for her collections, through a combination of creative styling, location, lighting, model selection and pose.

2

Illustration and graphics

Fashion illustration is a recognized art form and many talented fashion illustrators are held in high esteem alongside other contemporary artists. Fashion illustration changes and evolves as regularly as fashion trends do, and cultural changes impact the sort of art that the public responds to.

Fashion illustration has become increasingly stylized and, alongside conceptual fashion photography, has become more of an expression of the industry and the time in which we live than a record of what we wear. Digital design has also had a lasting impact on the media used to create fashion illustration and the ways in which those images are shared with others.

Timeline of modern fashion illustration

In the early twentieth century, what is considered by many to be the first true fashion magazine, Le Gazette du Bon Ton, was launched. It supported the new style of fashion illustration, with dramatic models depicted with personality and narrative encapsulated in their appearance.
The magazine is credited with launching the careers of artists and illustrators such as Georges Lepape, Paul Iribe, Romain de Tirtoff (Erté), and Georges Barbier.

In the 1930s, interest in fashion illustration grew and this period, during which photography was still developing, saw many opportunities for artists and illustrators to depict the latest trends. Artists such as Raoul Dufy and René Magritte offered their own interpretations of fashion.

In the 1940s, styles developed further and illustrators such as Carl Erickson (Eric) and René Gruau presented heavily brushed and inked charcoal impressions with loose lines and increased movement.

The 1950s saw the popularity of photography increasing, leading to illustration primarily being used in advertising campaigns. The 1960s and 1970s saw illustration further relegated to the realms of health and beauty editorial, as photography became more highly revered.

1   J PAULL MELEGARI

J Paull Melegari is a creative collaboration between Jacqui Paull and Carl Melegari. They work together to combine elements of illustration and photography, digitally.

1

2

The 1980s saw the birth of the new fashion press with magazines such as *i-D*, and art direction from the likes of Neville Brody and photographer Nick Knight. This explored new ways of communicating ideas and saw the development of a more provocative, street-style illustrator. Patrick Nagel began creating his graphic images, which spanned music promotion and fashion. Vibrant youth culture influences began to be reflected in fashion illustration techniques of this time.

The 1990s and 2000s saw the rise of the fashion illustrator once more. The multitude of styles, media and techniques employed is hugely varied, from graphic to the avant-garde, to digital and everything in between.

2 PAUL IRIBE

This illustration by Paul Iribe dates from around 1910 and depicts a woman wearing a dress by French designer Poiret.

Illustration and graphics

From graphite to pixels

Creating a graphic representation of a brand, and perhaps a character that represents its personality, can be a complex design process. As with photography and styling, there are many considerations to ensure the visuals clearly represent what the brand aims to offer the customer. Fashion illustration is also used by designers to show the development of a garment as it progresses from idea and inspiration, through testing and construction to manufacture and marketing. Most designers will show their ideas in a graphic format at some stage in the design process, and being able to illustrate ideas quickly is a valuable skill for all fashion designers.

There are a multitude of contemporary styles and techniques that can be used to show brand identity, garments and ideas in a clear, persuasive and creative manner. The characteristics of some of these are summarized below, together with examples of artists who use them.

Gamine

Identified by elongated limbs, this is a contemporary twist on more traditional illustration styles. Examples include Arturo Elena, Robert Clyde Anderson and Jordi Labanda.

Digital

Identified by clean lines, block colours, strong outlines. Examples include Béatrice Sautereau, Kristian Russell and Ed Tsuwaki.

Urban graphic

Identified by a strong attitude and narrative, muted colours, stance and expression of characters. Examples include Jamie Hewlett (co-creator of Gorillaz), Graham Rounthwaite, Banksy and Edel Rodriguez.

Fluid life

Identified by brushstrokes, fluid lines, traditional techniques, pencils and graphite. Examples include Egon Schiele, Garance Doré, Rainer Stolle, Aitor Throup.

1 'KIM'

This illustration by Michael Sibley depicts a life-like, photographic representation of the subject.

1

Childlike
Identified by shortened limbs, stylized child-like characters. Examples include Amy Davis, Yihsin Wu and Yuko Shimizu.

Photographic
Identified by life-like representations or combinations of methods (illustration and photography). Examples include Michael Sibley, J Paull Melegari and Carlos Maraz.

Manga
Identified by whimsical pictures and strong colours; this is a long-standing Japanese artform that has been embraced by other cultures and by fashion illustrators. Examples include Ben Krefta and Tezuka Osamu.

Other worldly
Identified by a strong ephemeral narrative, the background is as important as the figure, it can incorporate images that suggest a narrative. Examples include Genevieve Kelly, Frida Kahlo and Claire McMahon.

3-D sculpted
Identified by the use of materials such as clay or foam, which are photographed and manipulated. Examples include Liz Lomax and Seiko Ohmori.

Collage
Identified by the use of a mixture of media, often manipulated to create unique, sometimes distorted images. Examples include Christy McCaffrey and Claire Ann Baker.

2 'FLORAL STRINGS'

This illustration by Adele Page shows a slightly 'looser' photographic style than Michael Sibley's.

Video

Video has evolved into one of the most powerful tools for communicating ideas and messages and the ability to film, edit and upload work in the public domain has become significantly more accessible. The falling cost of filming, production and editing has seen many more videos being produced, as many people across the creative industries experiment with the medium of film, often for the first time.

A proliferation of brand and concept videos has been seen across the fashion industry. These have a longer shelf-life than a catwalk show, are generally cheaper to produce and have the added benefit of being able to reach a much wider audience. Some designers have replaced catwalk shows with film entirely, while others use it to share the catwalk experience with a wider audience, even after the live event is over.

1

Working with film professionals

Commissioning a fashion film, even a low-budget one, can be time-consuming and requires a very strong creative collaboration between the designer and the professionals involved. As most designers are not qualified in filmmaking, it is useful to speak to those that are, and basing a film project plan on their experience. Producing videos has become considerably cheaper with the introduction of digital technologies, but it is still a complex process to be involved in.

On a small budget, film professionals, such as editors, camera operators, directors and producers, can be sourced from colleges and universities that teach film courses, where students and staff may be interested in participating in film projects. Larger budgets give access to freelance filmmakers and large-scale film production companies.

Some fashion brands employ teams of in-house experts that continually produce content for online channels. Film companies that specialize in short online films have also begun to appear. Many designers have embraced the notion of fashion films and websites such as SHOWstudio, established by visionary image maker Nick Knight, which showcases the very best of contemporary fashion film. Short fashion film festivals and awards have also begun to appear, such as the Diane Pernet 'A Shaded View on Fashion' festival.

For new designers, fashion films can be an effective way to establish a strong presence and visual identity, if interpreted and presented in the right way.

Online magazine sites that represent brands, along with recognized online and offline publications, have a multitude of video offerings. Specialist YouTube channels have appeared in abundance, offering interviews and industry insight.

Working with film is not as easy as just pointing and filming, however, and while there is a place for amateur footage, there is still a strong desire from the consumer to see well-scripted, planned, filmed and produced video content.

**1 UNITED COLORS OF
BENETTON AW11**

Benetton uses video to showcase
its latest campaigns.

Video

Channels for promoting work

With the accessibility of online video content sharing sites such as YouTube, Vimeo and Flickr, opportunities for sending out films and promoting them are huge. A growth in consumer interest in video has meant that millions more people will now watch original and independent footage than ever before. However, this also means there are many more hours of film to compete with.
To create the right impact, it is vital to ensure the content, tone and style of a branded video is both appropriate and compelling.

Once the content is created and the audience identified, it can be shared on individual websites, sent out via links on social media channels such as Twitter and Facebook, and made available via video sharing sites, in the public domain.

Fashion films are often showcased at fashion weeks, and before and after the event through the organizers' websites. Many other industry websites also look for relevant content to share and promote.

Magazine websites now also often show videos, so these can be approached to see if they would share this sort of editorial content, if it fits with their audience demographic.

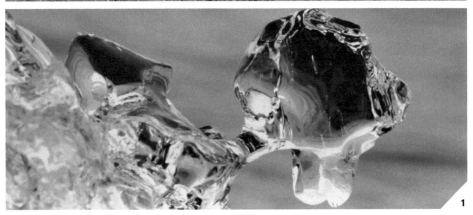

1

1   FERGURD, ICELAND

Stills taken from online
fashion video directed, filmed
and edited by Fabian Weber,
featuring designs by Ida Gut.

Web design visuals

Websites are now the first place most people will look to learn more about a brand and its products and services. Consumers now expect to be told everything about a brand on its website, and for the information to be up to date, easy to read and navigate, as well as being visually appealing.

As a key marketing tool, brands need to consider how their website will be found when people look for it on search engines, and how its ranking in search results can be improved – this is known as **search engine optimization** (SEO).

In the not-too-distant past, websites operated as a type of static online brochure that didn't allow for user interaction or engagement and could only be updated by web design professionals. The introduction of what is known as '**web 2.0**' has dramatically changed the way in which websites work and the ways in which consumers can access and use them.

Aside from brand websites, there are numerous other ways to create an online presence and communicate with audiences, from social media profiles and lookbook sites, to image resource sharing, apps and interactive media. Some of these areas will be covered later in Chapter 5, while this section will focus on the more directly branded online visuals.

KATIE EARY

HOME   AW12   DIGITAL POP-UP SHOP   <u>ARCHIVE</u>   FILMS   STOCKISTS   ABOU
SS12   AW11   AW10   SS10

SUNDAY 6 JUNE 2011

TIMOTHY
A NEW BOOK BY KATIE EARY AND
KRUSZELNICKI IS OUT NOW

"LONDON'S FOREMOST UP-AND-CC
DESIGNER HAS COLLABORATED W
PHOTOGRAPHER FABIEN KRUSZEL
CAPTIVATING STORY OF REAL TEE
LIMITED TO ONLY 200 HAND-NUME
TIMOTHY WILL BE SOLD AT COLET
AMONGST OTHER STORES, REFLEC
RISING STATUS WITHIN DESIGN CI

– DAZED & CONFUSED, JULY 2011

<u>READ+VIEW MORE</u>

WEB 2.0

Web 2.0 is the term used for the new wave of web applications that allow people to share information and collaborate online in a user-operated environment. Blogger sites such as Wordpress, social media sites such as Facebook and image-sharing sites like Flickr allow users to interact and collaborate with each other online. Whereas in the past software was located locally on a server or computer, these new platforms allow users to access their accounts wherever there is access to the Internet. New systems such as iCloud and Dropbox also allow the remote storage of information, files, documents, photos and contacts, so they can be accessed from a number of devices – phone, laptop, iPad – on the move.

1

SS12   AW11   AW10   SS10

SEARCH ENGINE OPTIMIZATION (SEO)

SEO focuses on how including certain keywords and phrases within the content of a website can improve its ranking in search engine results. Key information and words embedded in websites can affect how easily a website and its content can be found when someone searches for information, not just about a certain brand, but about a certain topic or word or phrase.

1   KATIE EARY

The Katie Eary brand website uses strong images and simple design to clearly showcase the brand and collections.

Web design visuals

Creating a website

Websites have become much more about regularly updated content and interaction than the static online brochures they once were. With the growth in blogging and the development of platforms that allow a novice to create an online presence, website platforms such as Wordpress have become comprehensive and user-friendly ways for even beginners to start to display their products, services, brands and information.

Website designers are increasingly using sites like blogging platforms to create a basic presence and then, if required, creating bespoke functionality and designs. This allows the client to update the site regularly themselves, without having to rely on – and pay for – the designer to do this.

Popular sites of this nature include Tumblr, Wordpress, and even micro-blogging or image blogging platforms such as Pinterest, and Instagram. All of these provide opportunities to create an online presence in a comprehensive format, for little or no financial investment.

1+2   HOUSE OF HOLLAND

Henry Holland's brand website uses strong visuals to showcase collections and features links to the brand's social media presence, including its Twitter account.

BRAND WEBSITE CONTENT

Most brand websites will include the following content:

× Lookbook – a library of images showing collections, current and previous, in date order so that customers can see the designs and their development.
× Videos of catwalk shows, stand-alone videos, and branded films.
× A profile of the designer.
× A brief background to the label.
× A press area with examples of previous coverage.
× A link to a blog which is updated on a regular basis.
× An e-commerce or shop function where items can be purchased, or links to sites where they are sold.
× Links to other relevant industry and designer websites, that the brand or designer recommends.

Creating a social presence

Complementing the more active, modern brand websites is the ability to further promote a brand and communicate with customers through social media. The micro-blogging phenomenon of Twitter can attract interested parties that may never have previously engaged with a brand. Photos and videos can also easily be shared through Twitter and other social media channels such as Facebook, LinkedIn, and Flickr.

These enable concise pieces of information about a brand to be shared with people interested in hearing about it in a less formal way than on a website. As social media encourages us to be more 'social' in the way in which we communicate digitally, it also gives us the opportunity to have conversations that we might not have had through more formal methods of communication, such as email.

Communication on social media channels is about more than just distributing business-focused information, it is about sharing with people. As communication becomes increasingly mobile, via smart phones and tablets, consumers expect to be kept up to date even more frequently and to be able to 'see' and engage with the people and principles behind the brands they support. It is no longer enough for a brand simply to have a slick website.

Case study: Poppy Roberts

Poppy Roberts is a young fashion illustrator, who graduated in fashion design from the University of Glamorgan, Wales. Having begun her studies in art, Poppy became interested in textiles and fashion and was drawn to the idea of being able to create and illustrate her own clothes.

Throughout her fashion design course, Poppy worked on her distinctive illustrative style and used this to create muses for her clothing collections. She also transferred some of her illustrative work into digital fabric prints. This process featured in her final collection, entitled 'The Deadly Florals'.

Poppy's philosophy is that art, and indeed life, is about enjoyment and expression rather than technicality and perfection. Her fashion design degree taught her that there is also a place for everyone within fashion, as it is such a vast subject and a huge industry.

Poppy draws inspiration from the poignant and beautiful work of illustrator Julie Verhoeven, as well as from a broad range of female artists from music, literature, performance, photography and painting.

Poppy begins the process of creating a new illustration by determining what sort of woman she wants to create. This might be influenced by something or someone that has recently inspired her, a certain facial expression, or an object that the character could wear in her hair. She then scours fashion magazines to find a strong pose to base her illustration on, and then traces a rough outline for a base figure to draw from.

Her drawings often focus on detail as opposed to form. She spends hours working on the face; melting watercolours all over the eyes and getting the eyelashes right. Facial expression is key to Poppy's imagery, as she wants it to communicate and relate to the audience. Once the detail is done through painting and drawing, Poppy scans the image and digitally adds various things such as flowers, string or anything that inspires her that week, using Photoshop.

'It's all about promotion – get online, get noticed, tell anyone you meet what you do and hand them a good, vibrant business card!'

THE DEADLY FLORALS

Poppy's distinctive illustrative style shines through in these images.

Interview: Jayne Pierson

Designer Jayne Pierson studied fashion design and has won the London Graduate Fashion Week Ecological Design Award. She gained a wealth of luxury brand experience interning and working for couture designers Alexander McQueen and Vivienne Westwood. Jayne regularly styles and designs for artists, musicians and actresses.

1

Q **How does the overall design process work for you and how do you get your inspiration?**

A It's a very personal story that I feel compelled to tell and this is the vehicle that I choose to use to tell it. However, this will evolve and the process may change. My inspiration is my muse who no longer lives in this world. I usually start with drawing and ideas evolve out of that. The dreams and everything else follows and I visually piece it together; sometimes I can't write it down quickly enough.

Q **Why did you start your label and what was the driving force behind the brand?**

A I was in my final year at university and in the middle of designing my final major project collection. I was still working at Vivienne Westwood and I felt the journey I had made through my internships and work at Alexander McQueen and Westwood had been hugely inspiring. Gradually, I learnt that there was a much deeper reason why these iconic designers design, and I began to understand the compulsion and the drive. During this journey I had discovered my story, my voice and I felt empowered that I had also discovered some of the tools that I could use to tell it. I applied to show at London Fashion Week half way through designing my final year collection and I was selected, so in some ways it was decided for me. However, when I had started I had no idea that this was where it was going to lead!

Q **How do you develop the concept for each collection?**

A They are chapters in her (my muse's) book. Each one follows the other.

'It's a very personal story that I feel compelled to tell and this is the vehicle that I choose to use to tell it.'

1   STUDIO IMAGES

Images from Jayne Pierson's Modrun Collection studio shoot.

Interview: Jayne Pierson

1

Q How important are the visual aspects for each collection?

A Very! I feel somewhat stifled by catwalk and the idea that only the guests invited can experience the show. I also find it confining to tell the story in that format. I feel far more comfortable with the medium of film as you can tell a story and a concept far more easily with so many more choices to make.

Q How do you use these films to promote your brand?

A For me, it's vital that buyers and press can view my concept with my collection and understand my thought process with the story and my muse. Film is the best vehicle for me in which to do that. I either present my film in a special event during fashion week or during my catwalk show. This can also be streamed live and can be emailed as a link after the event. Ultimately, many more people can share your vision through film than by just seeing a catwalk show.

Q How do you work with stylists and photographers?

A I do most of the styling myself as I design in looks. I also choose the models personally. Selecting the right photographer for each collection is also very important, as they need to see your vision as you see it, not a watered down version of what they want to do. I do have a group of creative people that I tend to work with time and time again as they have also become my friends and you find you get to a stage where you can instinctively know what each other is thinking and ideas spark and flow seamlessly.

Q Do you find it easy to communicate your vision to professionals when working with them?

A With the right professionals you find that you are on the same page from the outset and your references are similar, which helps communicating ideas immensely.

1 MODRUN STUDIO SHOTS

These lookbook images showcase Jayne Pierson's Modrun Collection.

2

Q How important is your web presence to the brand?

A Very much so, however websites are expensive and you have to work within your means, rather than not have one at all. It's important that the functions are clear and that it's all about the visuals.

Q What advice would you give young designers about creating brand visuals?

A Be succinct and summarize your message early on. Both good and bad branding are remembered, so think it all through and check your references before committing to anything.

2 MODRUN SCREENING

This screening, showcasing the Modrun Collection, was held during London Fashion Week in February 2012.

'Ultimately, many more people can share your vision through film than by just seeing a catwalk show.'

Exercise: Creating an illustration

Choose one of the ten contemporary illustration styles described on pages 104–105, and look for five examples of your chosen style. These can be taken from any source . Look at magazines, advertisements, posters, brochures, lookbooks, museums and art galleries – anywhere that displays imagery.

Once you've found your five examples, look at how they differ from other illustration styles, and think about the following points:

× What do you think are the key elements of this style?
× What do you like about the style? Is it the fluidity of the lines or the control?
× Is it normally a style that incorporates a lot of colour, or more muted or neutral tones?
× Could you recreate the style, but using an alternative colour palette?
× Does the style often appear in contemporary illustrations and advertising, or was there a specific period when it did?

Considering all of the above, make some basics notes and start to create an original fashion illustration in your own version of one of the styles you selected.

1 'RED SHOES'

Freelance illustrator Adele Page has developed her own distinctive style inspired by patterns and textures.

1

DIGITAL FASHION

5

The fashion industry has responded to the changes and opportunities provided by the digital revolution with great enthusiasm. As we've seen, bloggers have emerged all over the world, street style sites provide world trend feedback, and labels now engage with consumers in new ways.

The demand for new ideas in fashion has been propelled ever faster by the consumer's increased knowledge of the industry and trends, and the ability to instantly share this with others, on a global scale. Brands now have to consider the new nuances of promotion and marketing demanded by an ever more market-savvy and digitally-informed customer.

This chapter explores the ways in which digital communication has been embraced and developed by the fashion industry, and the impact this has had on brands, the media, customers and the very structure of the industry itself.

1 BRITISH *VOGUE*
   IPAD APP

British *Vogue* magazine now
makes its full print editions
available digitally, with added
features such as sound and video.

A changing industry

The digital fashion revolution is not just about fashion reporting or blogging. It has enabled new designers to create an online presence and increased exposure, giving increased visibility and new opportunities to engage with the customer. Armed with ideas, images, a well-developed brand and a well-designed and constructed collection, it is now possible to create an online presence and retail offering with relative ease.

Brands, including luxury labels that previously only experimented with digital channels and social media, now participate more frequently online. Live streaming of catwalk shows at fashion weeks has become commonplace, and followers can participate in and comment on events live, via Twitter.

Customers now have more opportunities to engage directly with brands, providing feedback and input that can influence the development of a collection. Marc Jacobs, for example, introduced a plus-size range, following direct social media feedback.

The fashion industry is built on mass communication – with a high turnover of new ideas and information, commercial exchange, visual stimulation and the development of brands and labels. Digital communication has essentially presented opportunities to conduct this communication ever faster, and globally, so it is little wonder that the industry has embraced new technology so readily.

2 NEW YORK FASHION WEEK

Models walk the runway for Fiona Cibani during SS11 Mercedes-Benz Fashion Week. Fashion bloggers are now as likely to be in the front row of such catwalk shows as the traditional fashion press.

1 POLYVORE

Fashion styling and blogging sites, such as Polyvore, are having a significant impact on the way in which fashion is reported and communicated.

2

A changing industry

POSTED BY YVAN RODIC AT 7:18 PM　15 COMMENTS　LINKS TO THIS
POST 📧

MARCH 27, 2012
KIEV - mercedes-benz kiev fashion days, day 2-3, 03/24-25/12

FACEHUNTER

MARCH 30, 2012
KIEV - mercedes-benz kiev fashion days, bonus 2

.ONDON - rose, tottenham street, 04/02/12

REYKJAVÍK - reykjavik fashion festival, day 3, 03/31/12

POSTED BY YVAN RODIC AT 8:23 AM　12 COMMENTS　LINKS TO THI
POST 📧

MAY 08, 2012
SYDNEY - fashion week australia, day 5, 05/04/12

MAY 17, 2012
SYDNEY - fashion week australia, bonus 3

1+2　FACEHUNTER

　　Yvan Rodic's renowned street style blog
　　can influence trends as well as increasing
　　the profile of designers, by showcasing
　　'ordinary' people wearing their garments.

1

The next generation of designers

'Generation-Y' is a term sometimes used to describe those born between the early 1980s and 2000. Also referred to as 'millenials', this group is characterized by a familiarity with communications, media and digital technologies. They have grown up with computers and mobile technology, and are comfortable sharing personal information and details online.

Young fashion designers from this group, beginning their career with an inherent understanding of new communications channels, may ultimately have a competitive edge in sharing ideas, designs, collections, thoughts and visions, online.

Many new designers use blog or portfolio sites, such as Viewbook and Pixpa, to promote their work and progress through their studies, long before they have a complete collection or a means to manufacture garments. Social media profiles contribute to the 'story' of a designer and their creative journey. Online videos or photo sharing sites further communicate a designer's sensibilities and vision. As such, it is now possible for a designer to build up an online presence and become highly visible to a wide range of audiences, before they launch a collection.

POSTED BY YVAN RODIC AT 11:32 AM   25 COMMENTS   LINKS TO THIS POST

MARCH 15, 2012
PARIS - fashion week aw 12, bonus 1

APRIL 26, 2012
ŁODZ - fashion week poland, day 2, 04/20/12

2

A changing industry

Influencing the fashion calendar

The consumer's constant demand for the latest announcements, trends and information has led to brands releasing collections more regularly than the standard two seasons each year. Some now offer online exclusives and early releases of their collections. Others offer exclusive deals and rewards to online communities and followers. The ways in which these collections are promoted and reach their markets is also being significantly impacted.

Events such as fashion weeks used to be something that only a select number of industry players, dignitaries and commentators would be able to attend. As we've already seen, since the development of digital content sharing and live video streaming, most catwalk shows are now available for anybody to view online, live and after the event.

The significance of this is that the consumer can now see new collections as they are launched, without having to wait for an editor and photographer to record and share them through magazine, newspaper or broadcast editorial. Consequently, the time for products to reach the consumer market is now considerably shorter. This also means the consumer can see the collections as they are presented by the designer, as opposed to seeing them once they've been mediated by an editor to suit their publication's target readership.

The consumer now has a similar, if not the same, level of access to new collections as the press and buyers do. In reality, many designers share new collections with 'official' industry players prior to fashion weeks, but the communication of brands has been shortened significantly through digital sharing.

The fact that consumers can now easily access a large volume of information about fashion brands, labels, collections and products, has also led some brands to offer additional collections to their mainline offerings, to keep the proposition new and continually trend-leading. Diffusion collections from luxury brands have also been introduced more readily as the general public becomes more familiar with these brands. Fashion brands have to continually explore new and innovative ways of personally connecting with the customer, to ensure they maintain market share and brand awareness.

venue   sponsors   buyers   media   contact

VANCOUVER FASHION WEEK
fall / winter 2012 | march 20th - 25th

Designers.

list of designers   designer profiles

Week has partnered with Foy Media Group
n March 21st at 6:30pm. In the meantime,
rmation. Click here to get the embed code

Profile: Justin Zachary

dreamed he would be a fashion designer. As a matter of
n acting in Los Angeles, California, when he stumbled
g that changed his life. Discovering that he had natural
ing and creating, Bartel went on to design sumptuous
ms and couture gowns, with an old Hollywood glamour
egance.

tail of both the inside and the outside of the dress,
hand, with the objective of having every women feel
ing that he would be designing couture gowns. Justin
e elegant timeless pieces for the sophisticated women of

ER FASHION WEEK   Designer : Soddi

Video Library

Video Library

blushing
boutique

VANCOUVER FASHION WEEK

Video Library

1   VANCOUVER FASHION WEEK

Vancouver Fashion Week, like many fashion
weeks, has a live video stream from the
catwalk shows that can be viewed online both
during and after the event.

Using social media to reach customers

1 ROBYN COLES

Milliner Robyn Coles uses her Twitter page to keep followers up to date with recent work, and to link to her website.

They key thing to remember when connecting with people via social media is that it is all about being 'social'. Brands that attempt to be too corporate and commercial in their social media activity generally experience lower levels of success. Communicating effectively through social media takes time, consistency, and an understanding of the audience you are trying to reach.

It is also imperative to share a little of yourself as a person, be it your interests, leisure activities, home life, work or thoughts. Used in this way, social media allows us to appear a little more human to each other, rather than just focusing on a work persona. The impact of this can be powerful if used effectively. For example, people on social media channels share information about themselves that they would be unlikely to give to a market researcher. This information – likes, dislikes, lifestyle, hobbies, and so on – can be gathered and used to send out information targeted at those that have already declared an interest in what you are offering.

For a small fee, Twitter, Facebook, LinkedIn and other market-leading social media platforms also allow brands to advertise directly to a carefully filtered group of registered users that have provided their location, age, sex, interests and other personal information.

The key to this is to avoid the traditional sales approach of bombarding users with the information that brands want to give them; rather, it is about listening to the consumer and giving them the information they want, in a targeted and appropriate way.

Community building is another key component of a strong social media strategy. If a fashion brand wants to build a base of loyal followers, they have to offer something of value to them. Many brands now offer appealing content to their followers on a regular basis, in response to their needs and wants. This approach means that when new products become available, the loyal fans and followers are more likely to be responsive to the occasional appropriately pitched sales-based message.

Social media allows consumers to make more choices about what, and who we listen to and how we receive information. A social media savvy brand will spend the time and commitment needed to build a loyal community of followers and fans, by listening to their needs and preferences.

'Smart companies understand today that good content – with an editorially-driven mindset, can be effective for driving positive customer engagements. The opportunity today is a media cloverleaf that spans tablets, cell phones, computers and televisions, and planning your narrative across different media channels is key'.
Steve Rubel, Edelman Public Relations

Using social media to reach customers

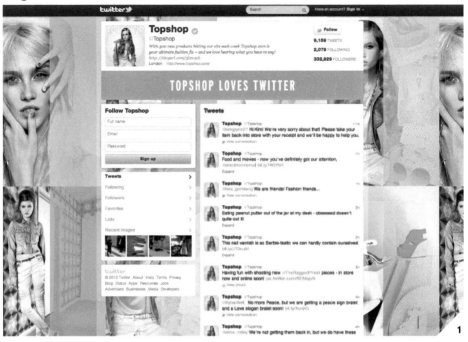

Navigating the social media landscape

With the plethora of tools, platforms and sites available, it can be difficult to choose the most appropriate ways in which to engage with your audience via social media. Some social media channels have been developed for personal interaction, some with a business audience in mind, while others are focused on engaging in a more consumer-driven way. It is essential to understand the demographic and functionality of each channel before engaging with it.

There has also been an increase in niche industry and activity-focused sites, forums, communities and blogs, which have sprung up to tap into audiences in an even more targeted way. Fashion blogging, for example, has become a huge genre for content creation and there are now many niche fashion blogs, focusing on areas such as vintage, street and celebrity style. Each of these meets the needs of groups of consumers who are looking for something directly applicable to their own interests, and brands must understand this before engaging with them.

1+2 TOPSHOP

Topshop uses Twitter to engage with its customers and give its large army of followers up-to-the-minute information on the availability of new products.

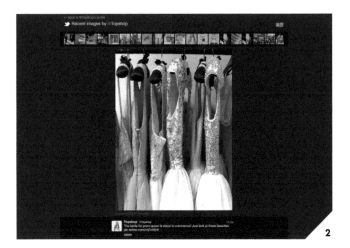

2

Sharing and collaborating

Sharing and collaborating through social media can have great influence. Part of the focus on digital communication is the need to openly share information and create content that is intended for sharing. Unlike traditional print vehicles, the focus for bloggers is about spreading the word through the sharing of text and images.

In essence, the consumer and reader become part of the promotion process for a brand – sharing information online, sending it to contacts and followers, until it is blogged and tweeted about. This online word-of-mouth activity can have incredible power when it comes to brand building.

In the fashion industry, where exclusives and trendsetting are an intrinsic part of how brands establish their niche, the consumer and content writer is focused on spreading the latest news, information and images before anyone else does. As a result, the reach of blogging, information sharing and collaboration is widespread and influential.

In some cases, there are still blurred lines in terms of copyright protection of original images and words shared in this way online. Some larger brands exercise strict control over the use of images and content to protect their brand equity, but many also accept that as long as the original owner of the content is credited, sharing is allowed and even encouraged.

Many blogs and content creators also actively participate in writing for each other, to spread their influence further afield and build a greater online presence. The beauty of being able to link each area of online presence and activity is that it can significantly build search engine optimization (SEO) and brand awareness.

Citizen journalism and blogging

Bloggers have been referenced throughout this book as they have had such a significant impact on how many consumers now read about fashion. Online information is now the most influential media for consumers. Blogs offer an accessible way to follow new trends as they emerge. There are now a huge number of bloggers across the world sharing their thoughts, opinions and news about fashion where they are, and across the globe.

Types of blog vary greatly, and while there are a number written by people not working in the industry, there are also many written by industry professionals. A significant proportion of professional bloggers have some previous media experience. So, although a blogger could be someone who writes for enjoyment and to share their personal views, many of the most successful blogs are actually written by people with experience in fashion, the media, or both.

TYPES OF BLOGGER

'Industry bloggers' are generally journalists and experts, stylists or employees of brands or publications. They tend to offer advice, trend updates, and suggestions of what to buy.

'Citizen bloggers' are passionate consumers of fashion. They share their own personal style, images, opinions, details of their shopping habits and where to find exclusives or unique items.

LEADING FASHION BLOGS

Some of the most high-profile fashion bloggers include:
- × ashadedviewonfashion.com Diane Pernet – industry blogger, filmmaker, editor.
- × stylebubble.typepad.com Susie Bubble – citizen blogger, fashion lover.
- × bryanboy.com Bryan Boy – citizen blogger, fashion lover, travels the world.
- × thesartorialist.com Scott Schuman – industry blogger, works in fashion marketing.
- × thestylerookie.com Tavi Gevinson – citizen blogger, teenage blogging phenomenon.
- × businessoffashion.com Imran Amed – industry blogger, business and management expert.
- × mademoisellerobot.com Laetitia Wajnapel – journalist, industry blogger, also has own styling site.

SCANDLUST ANNA DELLO RUSSO BRYANBOY DIESEL FASHION TOAST INDUST STYLE BY KLING

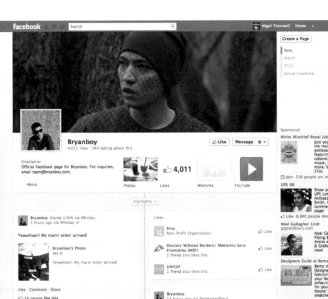

1 BRYAN BOY

'Citizen blogger' Bryan Boy has become very influential since setting up his blog in 2004. He is now a regular at high-profile industry events.

1

Citizen journalism and blogging

Street style sites

One of the most influential, widespread and ground-breaking blog formats to emerge has been the street style site, showcasing the personal style of ordinary people photographed on the street.

The significance of street style sites is that they champion the idea of a personal, inimitable style, which is not necessarily based on current trends. They also have supported – albeit unwittingly, perhaps – the idea that we can all take and share photographs that others will want to see, regardless of our experience as photographers or stylists.

Both high-street and high-end brands use street style sites as research resources to see what's being worn around the world, and also as their own vehicles to support the notion that the consumer has an influence on driving trends.

JAK & JIL

1 JAK & JIL

Street style blogs have become influential and can become well crafted photo-journalist style records of the time and style of a city or location.

1

Magazine-style brand sites

Brands looking to build an in-depth connection with the customer while competing with the wave of amateur content creators, such as bloggers, have begun to offer news, views and comment on their own editorial-led websites. High-street brand, River Island, created its Style Insider site to share fashion news and updates, along with details of products.

Luxury brands now also offer in-depth, regular content, as they are continually competing for the customer's attention and loyalty. The type of 'soft sell' approach these sites embody – encouraging the customer to visit brand sites for more than just purchasing activity – has become commonplace. Customers now expect a more rounded experience of a brand. Content is used to attract customers who then buy into the brand, and are more likely to make a purchase.

Amateur bloggers often collaborate with official branded sites, and employees at some brands are encouraged to build a more personal connection with customers through blogging.

This notion of employees conversing readily and openly with the customer on a personal level supports the idea that business has become more social and less formal in its communication with the customer. Brands are still exploring the possibilities this presents and discovering new ways of making social media conversation a more commercial transaction.

The future

**We have seen how digital developments have impacted every area of fashion promotion and communication.
Digital technology and communication will continue to evolve to meet the needs of consumers, and to allow brands to develop and compete with one another.**

Predictions about what will come next are regularly made, but one thing that is certain is that there is no going back in terms of how we communicate. Online sales of fashion continue to grow, and there are now many brands that sell exclusively online, although the physical experience of shopping is likely to continue to be a popular pastime.

Online-only offerings

Until recently, it was generally accepted that a fashion brand had to take a multi-channel approach to selling – it wasn't enough for products to only be available online; brands needed an alternative sales channel to truly flourish. However, many online-only brands are now flourishing and expanding to meet increasing demand.

Mass-market online-only stores, such as net-a-porter and ASOS, are highly successful but owe part of their success to the brands they represent. Most of these brands will have their own offline outlets, as well as conducting marketing and promotion. Other online stores, such as farfetch.com (see pages 30–33), work on a similar principle, but represent smaller labels stocked by boutiques. These small labels couldn't afford shops, nor to invest in their own large scale e-commerce site.

Being part of a co-ordinated, powerful online shopping brand that focuses on the marketing, communication and supply chain of goods, allows these brands to significantly extend their reach.

Emerging technologies

Fashion brands are exploring ways that new technology can expand their profile, build sales, and increase customer loyalty. From mobile apps to virtual reality, these present new ways to share content and also for the customer to pay for the items they buy.

High-street retailers have begun to focus on extending their in-store experience to make the same information available as can be accessed online. Online sales of fashion goods are still lower than in-store sales, but most research into what to buy is conducted online. Making that information available in-store will enable customers to combine the online and offline experience.

Virtual reality functionality, such as virtual fitting rooms which enable consumers to 'try things on' online, are also being developed. Fits.me have developed one such system, allowing online buyers to enter their own measurements to see how specific items would fit them. This increases sales and also decreases the number of items being returned because they don't fit.

Ways of making digital information available in fitting rooms are also being explored. QR codes are being used increasingly widely, allowing consumers to scan details of products and services with their mobile phones. New banking technologies are also allowing consumers to make payments with their mobile phones and through contactless technology bank cards.

The processes that lead to a purchase, and the ways in which a purchase is made will continually be challenged and reinvented as the possibilities of technology, virtual reality and mobile apps are explored and developed further.

1   FITS.ME

Fits.me is a virtual fitting room solution that works with brands to offer customers the ability to 'try things on' online, by adjusting the virtual mannequin to reflect each customer's individual measurements.

Case study: What Katie Wore

TAKEN ON THE WALK IN

1.06.12 | 7 comments so far - leave us another?

What Katie Wore emerged as a successful example of how much reach and influence a fashion blog can have if the idea sparks enough interest and the information supplied is consistent, unique and personal.

The blog was established in 2009 by creative couple Joe Sinclair, creative director at a global PR agency, and Katie Mackay, a strategist at an advertising agency. The blog was written by Joe and featured images of Katie wearing a different outfit each day. The idea behind the blog was initially to record the couple's daily lives in an interesting way.

Joe describes the reasons for setting up the blog: 'There were no lofty aims, or certainly no commercial ones anyway. Katie was complaining one day that I never wrote her any love letters. I thought that by writing each day about Katie's amazing technicolour wardrobe, along with snippets of information about our daily lives, I'd be forgiven for my otherwise unromantic nature. Plus, it would mean that Katie's mum and dad, who live in Scotland, would be able to keep track of what we're doing.'

AT KATIE WORE

AKEN BACK IN THE BIG SMOKE

05.11 | 8 comments so far - leave us another?

OWN

- leave us another?

WHAT KATIE WORE

TAKEN ON CHRISTMAS EVE

12.24.11 | 1 comment so far - leave us another?

're home! It was a relatively painless flight back from Bangkok so we're both feel
isher than we probably should. That said though, I'm writing the blog while Joe ha
perhaps it's just me who's winning in the battle against jet lag.

sing the thrill and mania of Bangkok, but have to admit it was lovely to pull out m
rdrobe when we got back from the airport this morning! Here I am just before I he
work in a gorgeous vintage dress from Another Timeless Place with Prada su
d a Mandarina Duck bag (a TK Maxx bargain).

e to be home

We've been out shopping in Singapore. It's been lots of fun. We've had some di
ght some stuff and then gorged on tonnes of dim sum. We fly off again tomorrow
e off to hit up Raffles for cocktails.

wears an ASOS dress, All Saints sandals and Chanel bag. The hairy creep t
vears ridiculous Micropacers.

e this: ❚ Like   ▶ Tweet 2

Would you believe this is the 3rd Christmas Eve for What Katie Wore? Amazing eh? It's
almost 3 years since I took the photo for the very first post (Katie looked well moody).

Hope you're all feeling very festive with a big pile of presents under the tree and several
drunk relatives quietly snoozing nearby.

Christmas Love. J&K

X

T KATIE WORE
KEN PRE PARTY
11 | 2 comments so far - leave us another?

T KATIE WORE
KEN ON BANGKOK DAY 3
1 | 1 comment so far - leave us another?

Although the blog wasn't necessarily set up as a fashion blog, people began to visit it to see what the inimitably stylish Katie was wearing, and it soon attracted an army of followers.

In terms of promoting the blog, there was no plan as it was aimed at just three people – Katie and her parents. Comments and requests from followers were responded to, and both Joe's and Katie's jobs put them in touch with stylists, directors and journalists, so the word began to spread.

The blog ran for three years, during which it was featured in almost every daily newspaper in the UK, along with dozens of glossy magazines. Katie was photographed in over 1,000 outfits, and seen by more than five million people.

Joe explains why he thinks some blogs attract so much attention: 'There's always room for good content, whether it's on TV, in print or online. What's been great about the explosion of blogging over the last decade is that it's created spaces for niche subject areas that would normally never warrant 30 seconds of fame. It allows people to be themselves and build communities with like-minded individuals, wherever they are across the globe.'

IE WORE
N AFTER THE CHRISTMAS PARTY
mments so far - leave us another?

ery good party last night, but today has been more than a bit of a struggle.
n for an early night on the sofa waiting for Joe to come back.

is been a good laugh, but I spose it's time to come home. We fly o
means we've still got eight hours to go for a last swim, have one l
he hotel bar like any good Brit abroad. See you tomoz in cold, gr
id.

ears a very regal ASOS dress and Mellow Yellow sandals from S

APPY BIRTHDAY JANE!

this: Like   Tweet 3

WHAT KATIE WORE
Images taken from the daily personal fashion blog of Katie Mackay.

JOE'S TIPS FOR SETTING UP A FASHION BLOG:

× Find a unique angle, tone of voice or positioning – and make sure it's one you can sustain over a long period of time.
× Host it yourself – for the sake of a small sum of money spent on hosting it, you will have much more freedom in the long term.
× Make sure your URL (blog address) is memorable and short.
× Get yourself set up on Twitter and Facebook and be sure to integrate them into the blog. These social platforms will be your main source of traffic.

Interview: Harriet Williams

Harriet Williams worked as a business analyst and management consultant in the UK, Europe and the US, before joining UK retailer Debenhams in 2007. She held a number of posts at Debenhams before becoming head of digital in 2010, with responsibility for increasing multi-channel sales through online marketing, mobile and international initiatives.

Q How did you become head of digital at Debenhams?

A I started at Caterpillar – originally, I was involved in selling construction equipment, so not your traditional route into high-street retail! My academic background is in science and I'm naturally analytical, but also enjoy being creative. I have had a number of roles at Debenhams and I found e-commerce and digital marketing is the perfect fit with its analytical and creative aspects.

Q What did the role involve?

A I'm responsible for online marketing, including search marketing, online display, and affiliate programmes. I also lead all of our mobile commerce initiatives, including mobile apps, mobile site, mobile pop-ups, QR codes, and augmented reality trials, plus anything digital that we utilize to promote our brand. We're quite innovative in the digital space. My final area of responsibility is expanding our e-commerce offer internationally.

Q How focused is Debenhams on developing digital content?

A We're committed to a multi-channel approach when communicating with our customers, which includes creating digital content and experiences. Fundamental to our future growth is extending our presence on an international level via multi-channel retail experiences, which will include the development of mobile apps and content as well as in-store digital experiences via touchscreen technology.

Q How important is it to have your own online content?

A We've recently invested in our own Debenhams TV channel, and we have our own magazine-style blog a Facebook community, and an online beauty club. We also trialled a Debenhams virtual pop-up store, where customers can 'try on' garments without even coming into the store. We're also launching an iPad app with a magazine section including fashion, and beauty advice. I guess you can say we are pretty committed to creating our own content.

1 DEBENHAMS DIGITAL

These images highlight some of the many ways in which Debenhams engages with their customers.

Interview: Harriet Williams

Q What has had the biggest impact on fashion, from a digital perspective?

A Online buying in the UK is now a much more mature industry when it comes to retail. Approximately 10–15 per cent of fashion sales are now transacted online, but over 50 per cent of purchases are researched online first, before buying in-store, so offering online content that captures interest and engages the customer is key. The activities that we believe will see the biggest growth moving forward are focused on mobile access and interaction. Mobile connection with the customer via apps, and interactive barcode scanning that allows research and purchase on the move, along with mobile social media communication of posts and images. You can already pay for retail items via your mobile in countries like Japan and Korea, and this trend will spread globally.

Q How did you monitor online activity about Debenhams?

A We're trialling various monitoring tools to capture information and stats about where our brand is appearing and what's being said. However, there still has to be a level of human monitoring involved to physically search sites and stats. We also use a lot of the free tools out there such as Google Analytics, TweetDeck, and so on. We also closely monitor our own website stats and trends to be able to determine what works best when it comes to promotions and campaigns.

Q How do you plan online advertising campaigns?

A Our online campaigns are split into two main types of activity – monitoring and promoting our presence via search and/affiliate programmes and straight forward email campaigns. Both of these activities often run alongside what we're doing in the more traditional channels, such as print and TV advertising. We work with various agencies on creatives and delivery of campaigns and we're always testing everything we do. The beauty of digital is that if a campaign isn't working or meeting expectations, we can measure it and amend if necessary and this can be done in real time. The virtual pop-up store we ran was a good example of one of our trials that we tested to see the response.

1 **DEBENHAMS STORE**

A Debenhams store interior – the future may include in-store touchscreens that bring online information into the offline physical experience of shopping.

1

Q What do you think is the future for digital fashion?

A Not many brands have truly explored the use of technology in-store as yet. The provision of touchscreens that allow customers to access information about products, purchase and arrange delivery whilst in store, along with touchscreens in fitting rooms that allow you to virtually try on items or find out more about them, is the way technology will develop. Shoppers still like the physical experience of shopping, but with the convenience of information available at their fingertips. We'll see this area develop over the next few years along with the continued development of mobile commerce.

Q How have you engaged with fashion bloggers?

A We have run affiliate campaigns with bloggers, where they receive commission if, through an advert or post on their site, they've driven traffic to ours. We also regularly invite them to our press shows, previews and key launches, and keep them up to date with what's happening. We ran an interesting campaign with Polyvore, a blogger community site, that encouraged fashionistas to create looks with Debenhams designer ranges. It generated a lot of great content and went viral as bloggers posted looks on their sites and on Facebook.

Q What have been the most successful types of campaigns to date?

A For revenue generation, the search and affiliate marketing campaigns have offered the best return. From an engagement and brand perception point of view, the mobile campaigns we run have been the most successful as they have brought in new customers.

Exercise: Fashion blog analysis

For this exercise, you need to conduct some research into current fashion blogs, by doing a basic online search to identify the top five fashion blogs in a given part of the world – Europe, Asia, the US, etc. Alternatively, you could use the list on page 135.

Once you have identified your top five blogs, spend some time reading through each one and looking at the features that they have in common, or that are different. Try to identify which blogs you think are the most important and influential, as well as those you like the best. What are your reasons for these decisions? Once you have got a feel for each blog, answer the following questions:

× What it is that makes these blogs so successful?
× How do they connect with their audience?
× What do you think are the most important elements for connecting with customers?
× How do you think the blogs have built a loyal following?

Use your answers to these questions to devise a plan for starting your own blog, if you do not already have one, or to identify how you could improve an existing one.

1 CARDIFF FASHION

A regional blog that taps into a niche, location-based audience. The site also attracts interest from the US, Australia and many other countries.

ESAH Menswear

2012 MAY 30

by admin

Welcome back to Cardiff Fashion! Have you subscribed to our RSS feed or email update service? Get new posts delivered straight to your inbox. Thanks again for visiting!

...new menswear brands on Cardiff Fashion, so it's always
...enswear range. ESAH (Exploration Starts At Home) Clothing
...ments made locally, incorporating graphic icons and imagery,

WWW.CARDIFFFASHION.COM

Fashions news, views & musings

Home   About   Links   Press   Hot Topics

Fred Perry Cardiff

1 COMMENT   2012 APRIL

by admin

Welcome to Cardiff Fashion! If you're new here, you may want to subscribe to our RSS feed or email update service - get new posts delivered straight to your inbox. Thanks for visiting!

They're a group of creatives with fashion, TV and film industry experience, and s...
work has been seen in Grazia, Look and Closer magazines. They say 'we like r...
producing striking and original imagery, teamed with intuitive design and precis...

Cardiff's newest young designers

2011 JUNE 5

...ff Fashion! Have you subscribed to our RSS feed or email update service?
...straight to your inbox. Thanks again for visiting!

...fashion designers, photographers and stylists around, have launched their
...capital this weekend, with the opening of the exhibition 'platform' at the ol...
...d Centre. Missing the opening and launch party on Friday night as I was ill...
...yesterday afternoon. If you haven't been in to take a look at this free show...

...se of work from students of the Cardiff School of Creative and Cultural Indu...
...wcases truly brilliant local talent. It's fantastic to see the amazing work,
...fashion that's evident amongst these creative young minds. But I'm going...
...... and over the next few weeks I'll be showcasing some of the individual
...enjoy!

...h them all the very best in their new venture and wanted to share some of their images with you...
...etails go to Brave New Media.

1

COLLABORATION AND CONNECTION

6

Collaboration in fashion can involve working with other creative people to help develop concepts, techniques or production ideas. It allows you to combine skills, share funds, and reach a wider audience.

Many designers find collaborating enables them to develop ideas further, enriching their creative process and final designs. Others find that combining skills keeps costs down whilst opening up new opportunities for brand exposure and investment.

Collaborative projects can also bring together designers that have the same principles about issues such as sustainability and ethical production processes. Ultimately, as with any industry, collaboration in fashion can simply be the coming together of minds to produce a superior product. This chapter explores the ways in which some designers work collaboratively and the benefits this approach can bring to all parties involved.

1 CELEBRITY ENDORSEMENT

High-profile celebrities often rub shoulders with top designers. Here actress Kirsten Dunst and iconic designer Karl Lagerfeld attend an event together, though ironically, Dunst is wearing Louis Vuitton.

Working with other industries

Fashion designers have long worked with a wide variety of collaborators to enhance their collections, attract investment and sponsorship, to capitalize on the influence of a celebrity, or simply to explore shared business or commercial interests.

Many fashion designers work closely with fabric manufacturers, as well as graphic designers and artists, on print and textile designs. Others have worked with architects on installations, partnered with car manufacturers on bespoke interiors, produced fabrics and materials for the home or become acting magazine editors. All of these activities provide new vehicles for building brand awareness and industry influence, and can provide designers with exposure to new audiences, opening up new sales channels for their products.

Collaboration and sharing

From a communications perspective, it is important to note that the growth in digital information sharing has also impacted the way in which designers and others involved in the fashion industry can work together and collaborate.

As we've seen, the notion of social media and blogging is based on the idea of sharing information. One influential fashion blogger may share information with thousands of people around the world, and they are likely to allow other sites and sometimes brands to link to their information in a sort of informal online editorial collaboration.

In the same way, designers are now sharing their thoughts, opinions and inspirations more readily with others, and can also access more ideas and information from around the world on the Internet. This interest in sharing information and ideas has enabled, and will continue to facilitate, even more collaboration among people with similar sensibilities and ideas of what the future of fashionable design is.

1 JIMMY CHOO/H&M

H&M collaborates regularly with fashion designers as well as celebrities.

2 ROELOFFS/VERSACE

Dutch artist Tim Roeloffs designed print images for a collection of Versace dresses. Both brands gained exposure and media interest, and the collaboration produced unique and innovative designs.

Working with other industries

1

Skill and style matching

Finding the right collaborative partner is key to the design process and to the end product. It is important to return to the original inspiration behind a collection or brand, when considering relevant partnering opportunities. Many designers come across like-minded potential collaborators through the course of their work and exposure to other industry professionals. Others actively seek out people or brands to collaborate with, choosing those that best complement their own design or brand ethos. Some brands that are looking to relaunch or re-energize their image will collaborate with brands or people that offer the desired kudos.

Designers have collaborated for decades with manufacturers, such as woollen mills and leather producers, highlighting the quality of materials as the focus of a collection, while endorsing the fabrics and the production techniques.

Australian merino wool, which had fallen out of favour as a high-fashion product in recent decades, has become a luxury material of choice for many new designers. A recent exhibition saw new Australian designers collaborate with the manufacturers of the material to showcase its use in high-end fashion. Australian designers Tina Kalivas, Josh Goot, Kym Ellery and Lisa Gorman made custom garments for the show that also featured Vivienne Westwood, Rick Owens, Burberry and Lanvin.

Collaborations such as this with complementary partners can be extremely powerful and create significant impact if both sides are committed to an agreed end. Ensuring the right research is conducted and goals are clearly defined at the outset is key to a successful partnership.

COLLABORATING

When considering who best to collaborate with, ask yourself the following questions:

× Which brand attributes would I most like to highlight through this collaboration?
× Which other brands and/or industries best match the focus of my brand?
× Have there already been similar collaborations?
× Which celebrities/artists/designers/manufacturers/producers do I most admire and want to work with?
× What have the people I most admire been associated with recently?
× How will the collaboration benefit my brand?
× What do I hope to gain from collaboration?

1 SWAROVSKI/LIGIA DIAS

Crystal brand Swarovski collaborated with jewellery designer Ligia Dias on this striking piece.

Celebrity endorsement

1

The increased popularity of reality TV shows, the growth in citizen journalism, the increased number of sales channels and the added focus on personal branding have all led to greater numbers of celebrities using their profile to endorse and sell products.

Brands that have a level of notoriety or appeal to the general public can be catapulted into mass-consumer awareness through the endorsement or support of a particular high-profile celebrity.

This has been shown through partnerships such as Madonna's collection created for H&M, or supermodel Kate Moss's collaboration with Topshop. Both of the resulting collections were highly coveted and sought out by high-street shoppers, keen to own an item associated with a high-profile figure. Whether a celebrity is actually significantly involved in the design of a collection is not necessarily of key importance – the consumer is more interested in the notional association with the style or image of the celebrity.

Fashion PR agencies work hard to encourage celebrities to wear clothes by the designers they represent, in the hope that they will be photographed in them. If an influential celebrity is pictured wearing a designer's clothes, it can make them much more desirable to the consumer.

1 M BY MADONNA

Window display of clothes from the M by Madonna range, produced in collaboration with H&M.

2

2 KATE MOSS AND TOPSHOP

Kate Moss promoting her Topshop
collection in-store.

Celebrity endorsement

1

Targeting celebrities for endorsement

Celebrities come in all shapes and sizes and it is important for a designer to target those that will best represent their brand, its attributes and ethos. There are a number of ways that celebrities can be targeted. Endorsement activity can range from them simply wearing garments, to becoming the public face of a brand, or working as the brand's ambassador by talking about and supporting it in public.

Celebrities will become involved with brands for a variety of reasons, including straightforward financial gain, access to free garments, an affiliation with a brand and its ethos, or simply because they like what the brand produces and stands for. Celebrities that are already managing their own personal brand will only endorse products that work well alongside it. As with any collaboration, there has to be mutual benefit for it to work successfully.

The latest reality TV stars can be just as powerful as more established celebrities when it comes to product and designer endorsement. They may only be in the spotlight for a short period of time, but they often attract very intense coverage in magazines, newspapers and online.

There have been some successful and extremely effective collaborations between designer and celebrity that have revived both brands and careers, opened up entirely new audiences for both parties, and provided brands with renewed influence and respect. The benefits of engaging in celebrity endorsement can be both significant and far reaching.

1   MADONNA AND JEAN PAUL GAULTIER

American pop star Madonna performing to fans in 1990. She and designer Jean Paul Gaultier collaborated on her iconic stage costumes during this period.

CELEBRITY ENDORSEMENTS

Celebrity endorsements are varied and don't always come about as the result of a pre-agreed collaboration. Kate Middleton, for example, openly supports British fashion designers and had her wedding dress designed by Alexander McQueen. The royal wedding, and many of the appearances made by Prince William and Kate Middleton, attract an international audience, which subsequently puts many British designers in the spotlight.

Michelle Obama, First Lady to US President Barack Obama, is also noted for the designers she chooses to wear, as has been the case with many previous First Ladies.

These sorts of endorsements or brand ambassadors, which often come about from a mutual appreciation, can have a lasting impact on a brand and how it is perceived.

Case study: DONT WALK

DONT WALK is a registered charity which runs a series of inspiring collaborative fashion events. It was set up by students at the University of St Andrews, Scotland, in the wake of the 9/11 terrorist attacks of 2001. Their intention was to raise money for those affected by the tragedy, through a celebration of the spirit and style of New York. The charity has gone on to support a number of other causes across the globe and has raised over £100,000 ($155,000) since it was founded.

DONT WALK holds events throughout the year including film screenings, talks and exhibitions to raise awareness of the work it carries out, among students and the general public. The events culminate each year in an artistic spectacle and fashion show, showcasing the best in student photography, fashion and design.

Internationally renowned, the eclectic fashion show attracts a mix of urban, high-street and high-end designers from across the globe. DONT WALK has worked with the likes of Yves Saint Laurent, Missoni, Barbour and the House of Chanel, as well as leading model agencies such as Next Model Management and Models 1.

FASHION SHOW

The 2012 DONT WALK catwalk show held in St Andrews in Scotland, which raised funds for African children's charity ZamCog.

The work of DONT WALK has been recognized and supported by a number of celebrity patrons, including Claudia Schiffer, Kate Moss, David Furnish, Alan Rickman and Dame Judi Dench.

DONT WALK has also received significant press support and coverage across a range of media, having been reviewed by publications including *Harper's Bazaar*, *Vanity Fair*, on networks such as CNN and the BBC, as well as by a host of specialist fashion and design blogs.

Each year the event is run by a committee of students who manage every detail of each activity, as well as the highly professional fashion show. Significant sponsorship is also sourced, along with the support of local companies and businesses, to ensure as much of the funds raised from the events as possible are passed on to the supported charities.

www.dontwalkfashion.com

Interview: Emma Griffiths

Designer Emma Griffiths trained at Westminster University
in London, before gaining industry experience with Alexander
McQueen, among others. Since then, her label E.G. has gained
coverage in magazines such as *Vogue*, *Harper's Bazaar*, and *Drapers*.

1

2

Q How do you find creative inspiration for each collection?

A Every creative is different, but you always have to have your eyes wide open, retaining images like a computer. I always carry a pencil and note pad with me so I can scribble down an idea when it comes. A lot of the time ideas for collections can cross over, so if I'm lucky, ideas for my new collection come to me when I'm finishing off the previous one. It's always inspired; it has to be. I have to surround myself with images and create a mood wall, then everything comes from there. I will always love the drama in opera, dance and art – but art I like, art that moves me or stirs emotion; anything that forces a reaction from me, even if its disgust. I thrive on the extremities of human emotion.

Q When was Emma Griffiths established and what's the main focus of the brand ethos?

A I guess you could say it's been an evolution of my life, in a way, but I finished studying in 2008 and began developing the brand then. The ethos of the brand remains the same now as it was then, with a strong, independent but feminine woman in mind.

1 EMMA GRIFFITHS

Collection image from the brand.

2 EMMA GRIFFITHS

Brand co-directors, Rachel Anthony (L), and Emma Griffiths (R).

Interview: Emma Griffiths

Q   **How important is it to work with other industry professionals, and why?**

A   Massively important, it's essential. I keep in touch with younger designers and brands and share as much information as I can. We Brits tend to keep information to ourselves which is pathetic – I want to see other people grow, too. This industry is tough; we don't need to make it tougher. I think you get what you give out, too. Be nice to each other – you know?

Q   **Do you collaborate/ work with other industry professionals for ideas and also production or manufacturing?**

A   I don't collaborate to get ideas as such. Collaboration is about the coming together of two or more creative brains and the one feeding the other. It's almost like helping one another in a way, sharing information.

'Collaboration is about the coming together of two or more creative brains and the one feeding the other.'

Q Are you interested in celebrity endorsement for your collections?

A You have to be, unless you want to get left by the wayside. You constantly have to change and adapt to the way things are moving. The industry changes and moves at such a fast pace, and you have to adapt to the world around you. That's just common sense business, but we are fussy – I can't abide these celebrities who are famous for nothing – I'm not impressed. I like the good old fashioned celebrities who were famous for being really, really good at something, you know – like people you admire for their talent, not the size of their chest or deriérre.

Q Is it important for a twenty-first century fashion brand to secure celebrity endorsement?

A Definitely. People identify with them – and certain celebs can completely embody your brand. The kind of women who work hard, and are top class in their field, whom women admire, aspire to be – they are the kind of celebs who can make you an overnight sensation.

Q How has digital communication impacted the way in which you communicate your brand to your customers?

A We are more accessible for our customers. Everything we do can be translated directly to the consumer, almost instantly.

Q What is the future for Emma Griffiths?

A World domination and nothing else!

Exercise: Corporate conscience

Consider your stance and principles when it comes to your
feelings about the environment, resources and employing people.
Do your views about these elements define your brand or are
they just considerations for you personally? Create a statement that
clearly lays out what your brand position is about these corporate
conscience issues.

'Benetton group is committed to being a
globally responsible company in social,
environmental and economic terms...'
www.benettongroup.com

**1 UNITED COLORS
OF BENETTON**

Benetton's clear stance on
sustainability and ethics is
integral to its brand identity.
It uses its global profile to
highlight causes, such as this
'micro-credit' scheme run by
co-operative credit society
Birima to help Senegalese
workers start small businesses.

Things to consider:

×   How you feel about production processes and
    the environment?
×   How do you want your brand and its designs to be
    perceived by the customer?
×   How and where are your garments made?
×   Where do you source your materials from?
×   Do you know how they are sourced/created?
×   If you employ people, how are you perceived by your
    suppliers/employees?
×   Do your garments make a political statement or are
    they considered controversial or subversive?
×   What sort of people would you like to see wearing
    your designs and why?

Once you have considered all of these elements,
think about how and if you will communicate these
to your customers. Are the answers to the questions
important to you and how your brand is represented?
Do you think they will be important to your customers?

MICROCREDIT AFRICA WORKS

UNITED COLORS
OF BENETTON.

BIREMA
Growing with microcredit

MICROCREDIT AFRICA WORKS **TOUSSO SOW LIVESTOCK MERCHANT** MICROCREDIT AFRICA WORKS

1

CONCLUSION

Fashion promotion and communication has experienced some of its biggest changes and challenges in recent times, and the opportunities to create and sell a brand have multiplied through the advent of digital media. However, at a time when almost every consumer is able to voice their opinions and feedback in a wider public domain via the Internet, it is still imperative for brands to be backed by a sound business idea with good products, responsive customer service and a clear understanding of what the customer wants.

This book has looked at the context for contemporary fashion branding and promotion, and how the developing world has led to changes in the economic landscape, impacting the reach and the ways in which brands sell and connect with their customers.

Fashion promotion, PR and marketing are now delivered through multiple channels, and the consequent need to develop a strong visual profile has been outlined.

Collaboration has been highlighted, as organizations continue to share information and knowledge for mutual benefit, work with other creatives for increased opportunities, and improve efficiency by reducing costs through joint ventures.

The industry surrounding the promotion and communication of fashion brands will continue to develop as the ability to provide and receive information continues to grow in reach and complexity.

Glossary

Affiliate programmes

Performance-based marketing that rewards 'affiliates' or 'partners' that bring new customers or visitors to the company's site or special offer programme. These have become more popular in recent times through collaboration with key bloggers.

Brand equity

The value behind a brand name that influences customer interest and response to the brand.

Bricks-and-mortar

A business that has a physical presence for the customer to see and engage with, a retail outlet or store, or a building for operations.

Citizen journalism

Content developed for public consumption, by people not employed professionally to write content. It most commonly refers to independent bloggers.

Collateral

Sales aids or materials used to provide further details about a brand or product. They include brochures, product sheets, lookbooks, web content, white papers, etc. These differ from advertising materials, in that they generally are used once the customer has engaged with a brand.

Cruise collection

An inter-season, ready-to-wear collection that is produced in between the two mainline seasonal collections produced each year.

Demographic

The statistical characteristics of a population which can include gender, race, age, location, etc.

Diffusion labels/collections

Secondary line or collection from a designer, that is generally available at lower prices than the mainline collection.

Live streaming

Multimedia (such as catwalk shows) delivered by a service provider, generally over the Internet, for an end-user to view online.

Lookbook

A collection of photographs or images to show the latest range of garments available from a fashion designer.

Mainline offerings/collections

A designer's main range of designs, or signature collection, that identifies what the brand stands for and is primarily recognized for.

Pay-per-click advertising

Online advertising that is only paid for once a potential customer clicks on the advertised link.

Point of sale

The point at which purchasing occurs, for example in retail stores. The term also refers to the promotional displays and materials used to encourage consumers to buy at point of purchase.

QR codes (quick response codes)

Barcodes that can be scanned using smartphones to directly link to online information.

Unique selling point (USP)

Something unique or different from a competitor offering, that sets a brand or product apart.

Virtual reality

Computer-generated environments that simulate the 'real world' or imaginary ones, for interaction and access to visual experiences.

Picture credits

p 3 styling and photography by Jayne Hicks
p 6 'The Teds', by Pooja Bahaar Shah
p 8 KeystoneUSA-ZUMA/Rex Features
p 11 Michelle McGrath, model Kara Campbell
p 12–13 courtesy of Topshop
p 14 courtesy of ASOS
p 17 Catwalking.com
p 19, 76, 122 Vogue iPad app Dec 2010, Condé Nast
p 20–21 www.my-wardrobe.com
p 22 Patrick Frilet/Rex Features
p 24 pcruciatti/Shutterstock.com
p 26 Moises Quesada
p 27 Wayne Tippetts/Rex Features
p 28–29 Hall Ohara, photography by Kei Ohnaka/ Takahito Sasaki changefashion.net
p 30–32 www.farfetch.com
p35 testing / Shutterstock.com
p 36, 54, 97, 106, 165 Benetton Group, www.benettongroup.com
p 38–39 courtesy of www.trendstop.com
p 40 © Serg Shalimoff
p 43 Dmitrijs Dmitrijevs
p 44 courtesy of www.mademoisellerobot.com
p 45 Alastair Baglee
p 46 courtesy of Vivienne Westwood
p 47 Rex Features
p 48 courtesy of River Island
p 51 Peter Scholz / Shutterstock.com
p 53 Beretta/Sims/Rex Features
p 56 (top) Nata Pupo / Shutterstock.com; (bottom) catwalker / Shutterstock.com
p 57 Nata Pupo / Shutterstock.com
p 58 design by Marion Hanania, photography by Estelle Hanania
p 59 KPA/Zuma/Rex Features
p 60–61 Images supplied courtesy of Mary Kay Cosmetics (UK) Ltd; ©Chris Francis Photography, www.ffotos.co.uk
p 62, 64 Julia Kasper, photography by Shelley Jones, www.milkandblue.com
p 62, 64 Model Lotte Goedhart
p 67 Elly Snow
p 69 vipflash / Shutterstock.com
p 71 lev radin / Shutterstock.com
p 72, 88 courtesy of Rebecca Gray; p88 ©Simon Thistle
p 74 courtesy of Liberty London

p 75, 86 courtesy of Fashion Press Week
p 79 Edizioni Condé Nast; photography by Steven Meisel; model Kristen McMenamy
p 80 Antonio V. Oquias / Shutterstock.com
p 81 GRAZIA UK
p 82–83 www.businessoffashion.com
p 84–85 Ania Maria Rózanowska ©2012
p 93 wittayamu / Shutterstock.com
p 94, 114, 115 © Poppy Roberts
p 96 ©AJIMAGERY
p 98 Nata Pupo / Shutterstock.com
p 99 Shelley Jones, www.milkandblue.com
p100 Michelle McGrath; photography by Nick Webster; stylist Kristina Ritchie; model Nicola Sargent
p 101 image by Jason Chapman
p 102 www.jpaullmelegari.co.uk
p 103 The Art Archive / Kharbine-Tapabor
p 104 Michael Sibley
p 105, 121 ©www.adelepage.com
p 108–109 www.fabianweber.com
p 110–111 courtesy of Katie Eary
p 112–113 courtesy of Henry Holland
p 116,118 Kahla Delahay for Jayne Pierson
p 119 by Ross Pierson
p 124 courtesy of Polyvore
p 125 lev radin / Shutterstock.com
p 126 courtesy of Yvan Rodic
p 129 ©VFW Management Inc.
p 130 courtesy of Robyn Coles
p 132–133 courtesy of Topshop
p 134 www.bryanboy.com
p 136 Tommy Ton/courtesy of trunkarchive.com
p 138–139 Fits.me virtual fitting room
p 140–141 courtesy of Joe Sinclair
p 142, 145 courtesy of Debenhams
p 148 Getty/Pascal Le Segretain/amfAR12
p 150 Ray Tang/Rex Features
p 151 Catwalking.com
p 152 courtesy of Swarovski; photographer Mitchel Sams; model Ocean Moon
p 154 Ray Tang/Rex Features
p 155 Richard Young/Rex Features
p 156 Daily Mail /Rex Features
p 158–159 © Celeste Sloman
p 160 © Emma Griffiths

All reasonable attempts have been made to trace, clear and credit the copyright holders of the images reproduced in this book. However, if any credits have been inadvertently omitted, the publisher will endeavour to incorporate amendments in future editions.

Useful websites

www.blogger.com
www.britishfashioncouncil.com
www.businessoffashion.com
http://carbonmade.com
www.colourforecasting.com
www.edelkoortinc.com
www.euromonitor.com
www.fashionmonitor.com
www.mediadisk.co.uk
http://pinterest.com
www.pixpa.com
www.prnewswire.com
www.promostyl.com
www.responsesource.com
http://showstudio.com
www.sourcewire.com
www.trendstop.com
www.tumblr.com
www.viewbook.com
http://wordpress.org
www.wgsn.com

Contributor websites/contacts

www.adelepage.com/blog
http://ajimagery.4ormat.com
http://bloodygray.com
www.bryanboy.com
http://cardiffcyclechic.wordpress.com
http://emmagriffithslondon.com/
http://esnow.carbonmade.com
www.fabianweber.com
http://facehunter.blogspot.co.uk
www.farfetch.com
www.fashionpressweek.com
www.ffotos.co.uk
http://hananiam.carbonmade.com
www.houseofholland.co.uk
www.in-process.org
http://jakandjil.com
www.jaynepierson.co.uk
www.jpaullmelegari.co.uk
http://juliakasperdesign.carbonmade.com
www.katieeary.co.uk
www.kahladelahay.co.uk
www.mademoisellerobot.com
http://michellevictoriamcgrath.com
http://milkandblue.com
www.moisesquesada.blogspot.co.uk
www.msibley.com
www.my-wardrobe.com
www.nickwebster.com
www.polyvore.com
http://poojashahstyling.carbonmade.com
Poppy Roberts – poppy1101@hotmail.com
www.robyncoles.co.uk
http://rozanowska.carbonmade.com
http://vanfashionweek.com
www.whatkatiewore.com

Index

Index

Acknowledgements

With special thanks

I'd like to dedicate this book to my lovely
mum, who was a brilliant person, a great
writer and a keen lover of books; all books!
I'd also like to thank my husband Craig,
my daughter Georgia and my son Casey for
all their support and patience whilst I was
writing this book and sourcing images.
I will take some time off now, I promise!

I'd like to thank all of the kind and inspiring
people who have contributed their time,
images and thoughts to this book, through
interviews, case studies, quotes, images
and advice. All of these people are busy,
committed and dedicated contributors
to the fashion industry and I genuinely
appreciate the time they have given me.

I would also like to thank AVA for giving
me the opportunity to put into words what
I have been carrying around in my head
for years. Special thanks to Leonie Taylor for
her picture research, Renee Last for getting
me started, and to Jacqui Sayers for her
unending patience and support throughout
the writing and image sourcing process.

The publisher would like to thank
Virginia Grose and Gemma Moran for
their comments on the manuscript.

BASICS
FASHION MANAGEMENT

Working with ethics

Lynne Elvins
Naomi Goulder

Publisher's note

The subject of ethics is not new, yet its consideration within the applied visual arts is perhaps not as prevalent as it might be. Our aim here is to help a new generation of students, educators and practitioners find a methodology for structuring their thoughts and reflections in this vital area.

AVA Publishing hopes that these **Working with ethics** pages provide a platform for consideration and a flexible method for incorporating ethical concerns in the work of educators, students and professionals. Our approach consists of four parts:

The **introduction** is intended to be an accessible snapshot of the ethical landscape, both in terms of historical development and current dominant themes.

The **framework** positions ethical consideration into four areas and poses questions about the practical implications that might occur. Marking your response to each of these questions on the scale shown will allow your reactions to be further explored by comparison.

The **case study** sets out a real project and then poses some ethical questions for further consideration. This is a focus point for a debate rather than a critical analysis so there are no predetermined right or wrong answers.

A selection of **further reading** for you to consider areas of particular interest in more detail.

Ethical: aware-ness/ reflect-ion/ debate

Working with ethics

Introduction

Ethics is a complex subject that interlaces the idea of responsibilities to society with a wide range of considerations relevant to the character and happiness of the individual. It concerns virtues of compassion, loyalty and strength, but also of confidence, imagination, humour and optimism. As introduced in ancient Greek philosophy, the fundamental ethical question is: *what should I do?* How we might pursue a 'good' life not only raises moral concerns about the effects of our actions on others, but also personal concerns about our own integrity.

In modern times the most important and controversial questions in ethics have been the moral ones. With growing populations and improvements in mobility and communications, it is not surprising that considerations about how to structure our lives together on the planet should come to the forefront. For visual artists and communicators, it should be no surprise that these considerations will enter into the creative process.

Some ethical considerations are already enshrined in government laws and regulations or in professional codes of conduct. For example, plagiarism and breaches of confidentiality can be punishable offences. Legislation in various nations makes it unlawful to exclude people with disabilities from accessing information or spaces. The trade of ivory as a material has been banned in many countries. In these cases, a clear line has been drawn under what is unacceptable.

But most ethical matters remain open to debate, among experts and lay-people alike, and in the end we have to make our own choices on the basis of our own guiding principles or values. Is it more ethical to work for a charity than for a commercial company? Is it unethical to create something that others find ugly or offensive?

Specific questions such as these may lead to other questions that are more abstract. For example, is it only effects on humans (and what they care about) that are important, or might effects on the natural world require attention too?

Is promoting ethical consequences justified even when it requires ethical sacrifices along the way? Must there be a single unifying theory of ethics (such as the Utilitarian thesis that the right course of action is always the one that leads to the greatest happiness of the greatest number), or might there always be many different ethical values that pull a person in various directions?

As we enter into ethical debate and engage with these dilemmas on a personal and professional level, we may change our views or change our view of others. The real test though is whether, as we reflect on these matters, we change the way we act as well as the way we think. Socrates, the 'father' of philosophy, proposed that people will naturally do 'good' if they know what is right. But this point might only lead us to yet another question: *how do we know what is right?*

You
What are your ethical beliefs?

Central to everything you do will be your attitude to people and issues around you. For some people, their ethics are an active part of the decisions they make every day as a consumer, a voter or a working professional. Others may think about ethics very little and yet this does not automatically make them unethical. Personal beliefs, lifestyle, politics, nationality, religion, gender, class or education can all influence your ethical viewpoint.

Using the scale, where would you place yourself? What do you take into account to make your decision? Compare results with your friends or colleagues.

Your client
What are your terms?

Working relationships are central to whether ethics can be embedded into a project, and your conduct on a day-to-day basis is a demonstration of your professional ethics. The decision with the biggest impact is whom you choose to work with in the first place. Cigarette companies or arms traders are often-cited examples when talking about where a line might be drawn, but rarely are real situations so extreme. At what point might you turn down a project on ethical grounds and how much does the reality of having to earn a living affect your ability to choose?

Using the scale, where would you place a project? How does this compare to your personal ethical level?

01 02 03 04 05 06 07 08 09 10   01 02 03 04 05 06 07 08 09 10

Your specifications
What are the impacts of your materials?

In relatively recent times, we are learning that many natural materials are in short supply. At the same time, we are increasingly aware that some man-made materials can have harmful, long-term effects on people or the planet. How much do you know about the materials that you use? Do you know where they come from, how far they travel and under what conditions they are obtained? When your creation is no longer needed, will it be easy and safe to recycle? Will it disappear without a trace? Are these considerations your responsibility or are they out of your hands?

Using the scale, mark how ethical your material choices are.

Your creation
What is the purpose of your work?

Between you, your colleagues and an agreed brief, what will your creation achieve? What purpose will it have in society and will it make a positive contribution? Should your work result in more than commercial success or industry awards? Might your creation help save lives, educate, protect or inspire? Form and function are two established aspects of judging a creation, but there is little consensus on the obligations of visual artists and communicators toward society, or the role they might have in solving social or environmental problems. If you want recognition for being the creator, how responsible are you for what you create and where might that responsibility end?

Using the scale, mark how ethical the purpose of your work is.

01 02 03 04 05 06 07 08 09 10

01 02 03 04 05 06 07 08 09 10

Working with ethics

One aspect of fashion management that raises an ethical dilemma is how to tackle the issue of cheap replica goods. Counterfeit products flood markets on the back of successfully marketed brands. Fraudsters can copy and reproduce new products so quickly that fakes are often available before the original. Brand designers can add specialist detailing to help identify a genuine product, but consumers do not necessarily notice it. Research shows that over 70 per cent of British consumers would knowingly purchase counterfeit clothing or footwear if the price and quality were acceptable. People often see counterfeiting as a victimless crime in which the seller is purely saving consumers from over-priced products sold by rich companies. How much responsibility should a fashion manager take when imitations are produced by unscrupulous manufacturers and demand is driven by consumers? Even if fashion managers wish to eliminate the trade of counterfeit brands, what might they most usefully do?

In 1955, Mary Quant opened Bazaar on King's Road, London. Situated in the Royal Borough of Kensington and Chelsea, the local clientele were wealthy young professionals, artists and actors. It was one of the first boutiques of its kind, stocked with new and interesting clothes targeted at the youth market. Its success drove Quant to create her own audacious designs that played with conventions, including the miniskirt.

Skirts had been getting shorter since the late 1950s – a development Quant considered to be practical and liberating. Although short skirts were also created by other designers, it was Quant who coined the term 'miniskirt' and it became an emblem of rebellion for the post-war generation who rejected the beliefs of their parents. With hemlines as high as eight inches above the knee, the miniskirt was, for many, a celebration of women's pride and assertion. But for others, it gave the impression that the wearers were sexually available and served to objectify women for voyeuristic men.

Alongside her designs, Quant created a recognizable brand identity featuring a daisy logo and countless images of her distinctive hairstyle. By 1966, she was working with numerous manufacturers and the commercial appeal of her lines enabled Quant to secure deals with American chain stores. In Britain, Quant set up her own label, which was available across 160 department stores.

The miniskirt of the swinging '60s stayed in vogue until the end of the decade. The Society for the Preservation of the Miniskirt demonstrated outside Christian Dior's fashion show because the collection featured a return to long coats and dresses but as the Vietnam War escalated, and the future looked less positive, the miniskirt fell out of fashion. Hemlines came back down to the ankle in a maxi style.

In 1966, the president of Tunisia announced that miniskirts were to be legally banned and other nations followed suit. In some countries, the wearing of hot pants has been held to constitute a judicial incitement to rape and in 2000 miniskirts were outlawed in Swaziland because it was believed that wearing them encouraged the spread of AIDS. More recently, in 2010, the mayor of an Italian beach town ordered police officers to fine women wearing miniskirts as part of their battle to 'restore urban decorum and facilitate better civil co-existence'.

Is it unethical to create clothing that makes women look sexually appealing?

Would you allow your young daughter to wear a miniskirt?

Is commercial success in fashion based on design or the ability to create a brand and negotiate business deals?

I believe in that one-on-one sell. I don't really believe in flooding the market with loads of goods that don't mean much.

Alexander McQueen

AIGA
Design Business and Ethics
2007, AIGA

Eaton, Marcia Muelder
Aesthetics and the Good Life
1989, Associated University Press

Ellison, David
Ethics and Aesthetics in European Modernist Literature:
From the Sublime to the Uncanny
2001, Cambridge University Press

Fenner, David E W (Ed)
Ethics and the Arts:
An Anthology
1995, Garland Reference Library of Social Science

Gini, Al and Marcoux, Alexei M
Case Studies in Business Ethics
2005, Prentice Hall

McDonough, William and Braungart, Michael
Cradle to Cradle:
Remaking the Way We Make Things
2002, North Point Press

Papanek, Victor
Design for the Real World:
Making to Measure
1972, Thames & Hudson

United Nations Global Compact
The Ten Principles
www.unglobalcompact.org/AboutTheGC/TheTenPrinciples/index.html